SOCIAL SCIENCE
PRIMARY 5

BY ME

Pupils are reminded that they should not write in this book.

SOCIAL SCIENCE
PRIMARY 5

			ANALYSE AND ORGANISE
	Getting started	Page 4	
1	**The Universe**	Page 6	Graphic organiser and exam preparation
2	**Representing the Earth**	Page 22	Graphic organiser and exam preparation
3	**Climate and weather**	Page 38	Graphic organiser and exam preparation
	Teamwork	Page 52	Cooperative learning project: Climate change
	Term 1 review	Page 54	Revision of term 1
4	**Spain's politics and culture**	Page 56	Graphic organiser and exam preparation
5	**Spanish population**	Page 70	Graphic organiser and exam preparation
6	**Europe**	Page 84	Graphic organiser and exam preparation
	Teamwork	Page 98	Cooperative learning project: Population problems
	Term 2 review	Page 100	Revision of term 2
7	**The Middle Ages**	Page 102	Graphic organiser and exam preparation
8	**Spain in the 15th and 16th centuries**	Page 118	Graphic organiser and exam preparation
9	**Spain in the 17th and 18th centuries**	Page 132	Graphic organiser and exam preparation
	Teamwork	Page 146	Cooperative learning project: Spain's history
	Term 3 review	Page 148	Revision of term 3
	Study skills texts & Unit review summaries	Page 150	Texts for comparative reading and pair-reading activities. Unit contents in point form for summary writing

CONTENT		SCIENCE PROJECT	FRAGILE WORLD	REVISE
• Celestial bodies in the Universe • The Solar System	• The Earth • The Moon	Build a planetarium	Space debris	Study skills Review of Unit 1
• The spheres of the Earth • Cartography	• Landforms and weather • Globes and world maps	From A to B	GPS	Study skills Review of Unit 2
• What affects climate? • Climate zones	• Climates in Spain	Make a climate graph	Climate change	Study skills Review of Unit 3
• The Constitution • How is Spain organised?	• Autonomous Communities	Class elections	Democracy	Study skills Review of Unit 4
• Our changing population • Characteristics of the Spanish population	• Migrations in Spain	Population pyramids	Migration	Study skills Review of Unit 5
• The population of Europe • The European Union	• How the EU is organised	Countries of the EU	Rights of EU citizens	Study skills Review of Unit 6
• Al-Andalus • Christian Kingdoms	• Medieval cities • Art in the Middle Ages	The City of Three Cultures	Muslims, Jews and Christians	Study skills Review of Unit 7
• The Catholic Monarchs • The discovery of America	• The Spanish Empire	Spanish Renaissance	A cultural rebirth	Study skills Review of Unit 8
• Spain in the 17th century • The Golden Age	• Spain in the 18th century	Analysing a painting	The poor and the rich	Study skills Review of Unit 9

Getting started

Look at the three photos. What are you going to learn about this year?

Imagine a world without Social Science!
Read and discuss.

Social Science helps us understand the society we live in. It teaches us about the community and the relationships between individuals. Social Science shows us how geographic, economic, political and historical factors influence our lives. It also teaches us to respect social norms and democratic values.

The Earth is unique compared to other planets; it is the only planet known to support life. A variety of scientists work constantly to understand the complex processes that occur on our planet.

1. What do these scientists study?
   - astronomers
   - archaeologists
   - meteorologists
   - cartographers
   - geologists
   - biologists
2. How many types of maps can you think of? Explain how each one is useful.
3. Describe how climate affects your life.

Spain is one of the 28 members of the European Union. It is a democratic country where citizens' rights and responsibilities are defined in the Constitution.

1. Which countries do you associate with these words?
   - Colosseum
   - tulips
   - Dublin
   - Helsinki
   - Shakespeare
   - Copernicus
   - Louvre Museum
   - fjords
   - Mozart
   - Budapest
2. How many inhabitants does Spain have?
3. What are some languages that inhabitants of the EU speak?

The year 1492 marked the beginning of the Early Modern Age in Spain. It brought the end of the Reconquista and the beginning of the Spanish Empire.

1. What happened in 1492? Choose the correct answer.
   - The Romans completed their conquest of the Iberian Peninsula.
   - Christopher Columbus discovered America.
   - The Muslims invaded the Iberian Peninsula.
2. How did the world change after 1492?
3. Identify these changes as positive or negative. Justify your answers.

1 The Universe

① Read and discover.

Life on Earth would not exist without the Sun. The Sun is our main source of light and heat. It is also the most important factor in producing weather.

The Sun is a very active star. During periods of high activity, the Sun emits huge amounts of energy in solar storms. These explosions of energy can damage satellites orbiting the Earth and even produce power cuts in our homes. Solar storms also create the auroras. What is an aurora?

(2) Why is the Sun important?

(3) What are solar storms?

(4) Sunlight is one of the conditions necessary in the process of photosynthesis. During this process, plants produce chemical energy. What do you think would happen to life on Earth if plants didn't receive sunlight?

(5) What might happen if satellites orbiting the Earth were damaged? Consider the consequences of damage to the different types of satellites:

- weather satellites
- navigation satellites
- communications satellites

(6) There are two types of aurora: aurora borealis and aurora australis. What is the main difference between them?

Analyse and organise

1 Scientific advances have made it possible for us to travel to the Moon and to study planets and distant stars. In your notebook, complete the table using the words in the box.

• space rocket • planetarium • telescope • astronauts • Earth • weather

.....	A vehicle used to launch people or objects into space.
space probe	An unmanned space vehicle designed to obtain scientific information from other planets or from outer space and transmit it back to ..... by radio.
artificial satellite	A man-made object which is launched into space and orbits the Earth or another planet in the Solar System. It can be used for TV and telephone communications, GPS, ... forecasts or map-making.
space station	A huge spacecraft which orbits the Earth and where ..... can live and do research for long periods.
.....	An instrument used to view distant objects, such as planets and stars.
.....	A building where the images of the night sky are shown.

2 Look at the photos below and identify the scientific advances from Activity 1.

a

b

c

d

e

f

③ Read the text and decide if the sentences below are true or false.

Space missions

- **1961:** Yuri Gagarin, a Russian, became the first human to travel into space. He orbited the Earth in the spacecraft Vostok 1.
- **1969:** The astronaut Neil Armstrong became the first person to walk on the Moon. The astronauts on his spacecraft, Apollo 11, had several tasks, such as collecting samples of lunar rocks and soil, examining the Moon's surface and taking photos.
- **1971:** The Soviet Union launched the world's first space station, Salyut 1. A three-man crew lived in the station for 22 days.
- **1973:** The United States sent its first space station, Skylab, the largest laboratory ever placed in Earth's orbit.
- **1977:** Space probes Voyager 1 and Voyager 2 were launched to study Jupiter and Saturn. They have made many discoveries, such as finding 22 new natural satellites and Jupiter's rings. Voyager 1 is now so far away that it has reached the outer limits of the Solar System.

a. Voyager 1 and Voyager 2 orbit the Earth.

b. Rock and soil samples from the Moon were collected by the crew of Apollo 11.

c. The first space station, Salyut 1, was launched in 1961.

d. Yuri Gagarin discovered Jupiter's rings.

④ Listen to the recording about the Hubble Space Telescope. In your notebook, complete the missing information.

- Like other telescopes, the Hubble Telescope is made up of .....
- It was launched into space in .....
- It orbits the Earth every .....
- It receives radiation which is not blocked by .....

Celestial bodies in the Universe

What is bigger: a star or a galaxy?

The **Universe** includes planets, stars, solar systems and galaxies. No one knows exactly how big the Universe is.

There are many theories about how the Universe was formed. Most scientists think that the Universe was the result of a giant explosion called the **Big Bang**. After the Big Bang, the matter in the Universe started to group together to form the different **celestial bodies**.

Stars are huge balls of gas where nuclear reactions take place. These reactions produce enormous amounts of light and heat. Stars are classified by three characteristics: colour, luminosity and size.

A **constellation** is a group of stars which make an imaginary shape in the night sky. Some constellations, such as the Great Bear, are named according to their perceived shape.

A **galaxy** is an enormous system of stars, dust and gas that is held together by the force of gravity. Galaxies can have different shapes: **spiral**, **elliptical** or **irregular**. There are billions of galaxies in the Universe. Our solar system is one tiny part of a spiral galaxy called the **Milky Way**. All galaxies are constantly moving through space.

Galaxies group together forming bigger structures called **galaxy clusters**. A galaxy cluster consists of hundreds or even thousands of galaxies.

A spiral galaxy

An elliptical galaxy

An irregular galaxy

The Great Bear is a constellation.

Other celestial bodies

Planets and **dwarf planets** are celestial bodies that orbit a star and do not emit light. Some planets have **satellites** in their orbit, which do not emit light either. Pluto is classified as a dwarf planet.

A **comet** is made of ice, dust and gases. Comets come from areas of the Solar System beyond Neptune and orbit the Sun in **elongated ellipses**. A comet has a **nucleus**, a **coma** and a bright **tail** which always points away from the Sun. The coma and the tail form as the Sun melts the nucleus.

Meteoroids are small pieces of rock or metal from an asteroid or comet that orbits the Sun. When a meteoroid passes through the Earth's atmosphere, it burns. This burning rock is a **meteor**, also called a **shooting star**. At certain times of the year we can see **meteor showers**. The pieces of meteor which hit the Earth's surface are called **meteorites**.

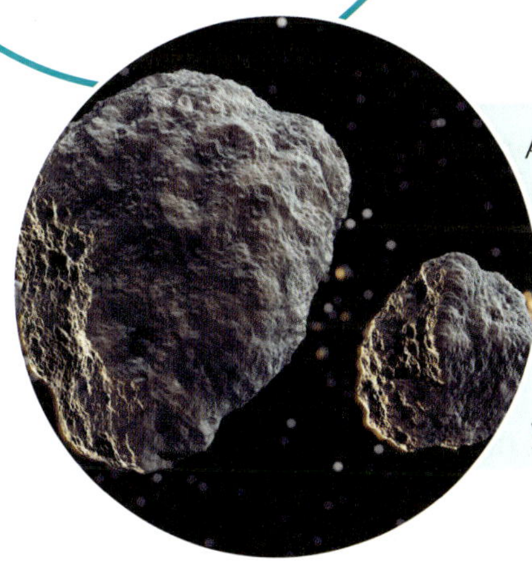

An **asteroid** is a rocky, irregular mass that orbits the Sun. Some asteroids are the size of small stones, but others can be bigger than a dwarf planet. Most asteroids take three to six years to orbit the Sun.

1. **In your notebook, order the parts of the Universe from the smallest to the largest.**

   galaxy — Solar System — Sun — Earth — Universe — galaxy cluster — Moon

2. **Explain the difference between a meteor and a meteorite.**

3. **Decide if the sentences below are true or false.**

   a. An asteroid is made of ice, dust and gases and has a bright tail pointing away from the Sun.

   b. We classify stars according to their shape.

   c. Planets and dwarf planets do not emit their own light.

   d. Some stars can also be shooting stars.

The Solar System

The **Solar System** is located at the edge of the Milky Way. It is made up of the Sun and the celestial bodies that orbit it: planets, natural satellites, asteroids, comets and meteoroids.

Celestial bodies in the Solar System

The **Sun** is a star at the centre of the Solar System. It is a huge ball made up of gases, mostly of hydrogen and helium. The Sun is about 110 times larger than the Earth. Like other stars, the Sun **rotates** on its axis. It also **revolves** (orbits) around the centre of the Milky Way. It takes the Sun about 220 million years to complete one orbit.

The eight **planets** that orbit the Sun are classified into two groups:

- Mercury, Venus, Earth and Mars are **inner planets**. They are solid and have a rocky surface. They are warmer and smaller than the outer planets.
- Jupiter, Saturn, Uranus and Neptune are **outer planets**. These planets are cold and dark because they are far from the Sun. They are called **gas giants** because they are made up of gases. All the outer planets have rings and many moons.

Most of the **asteroids** in the Solar System are found in two regions: in the asteroid belt, between Mars and Jupiter, and the Kuiper Belt, beyond Neptune.

Natural satellites orbit some of the planets. They are also called **moons**. Earth has only one natural satellite, but some planets have more than one.

Geocentric and heliocentric models

Our understanding of the shape and size of the Universe has changed over time together with advances in technology.

Ancient Greeks believed that the Earth was at the centre of the Universe. According to this **geocentric model** ('earth-centred') the Sun, Moon, planets and stars orbit the Earth.

In the 16th century, Nicolaus Copernicus suggested that, in reality, the Earth and other planets orbit the Sun: a **heliocentric model** ('sun-centred'). Around 100 years later, Galileo used a telescope to support Copernicus' theory.

Look at the picture of the Solar System. Which planet is closest to the Sun?

Did you know?

Halley's Comet is the best-known comet. It can be seen from the Earth every 76 years. The last time was in 1986.

When will we see it again?

1. What do these sentences refer to?
   a. It is the biggest planet in the Solar System.
   b. They can be found in the Kuiper Belt.
   c. According to this theory, the Earth is at the centre of the Universe.
   d. It is the only star in the Solar System.
   e. This person proved the heliocentric theory.

2. Find out more about the geocentric theory. Draw a picture showing the geocentric model of the Universe. Compare it with the picture of the Solar System above.

3. Explain the difference between a natural satellite and an artificial satellite.

The Earth

When do the four seasons start and end?

The Earth is the only planet where life has been found. From space, the Earth looks blue. This is because about 75% of the surface of the planet is water. The Earth moves in two different ways: it orbits the Sun and it rotates on its axis.

The Earth's rotation

The Earth rotates anticlockwise on its axis. Earth's axis is an imaginary line that goes from the North Pole to the South Pole. This line is not perfectly vertical. It is tilted at about 23 degrees. It takes 24 hours for the Earth to complete one rotation. This rotation gives us **day** and **night**.

Did you know?

In a darkened room shine a torch onto a globe. Spin the globe slowly anticlockwise.

Where is it day? Where is it night?

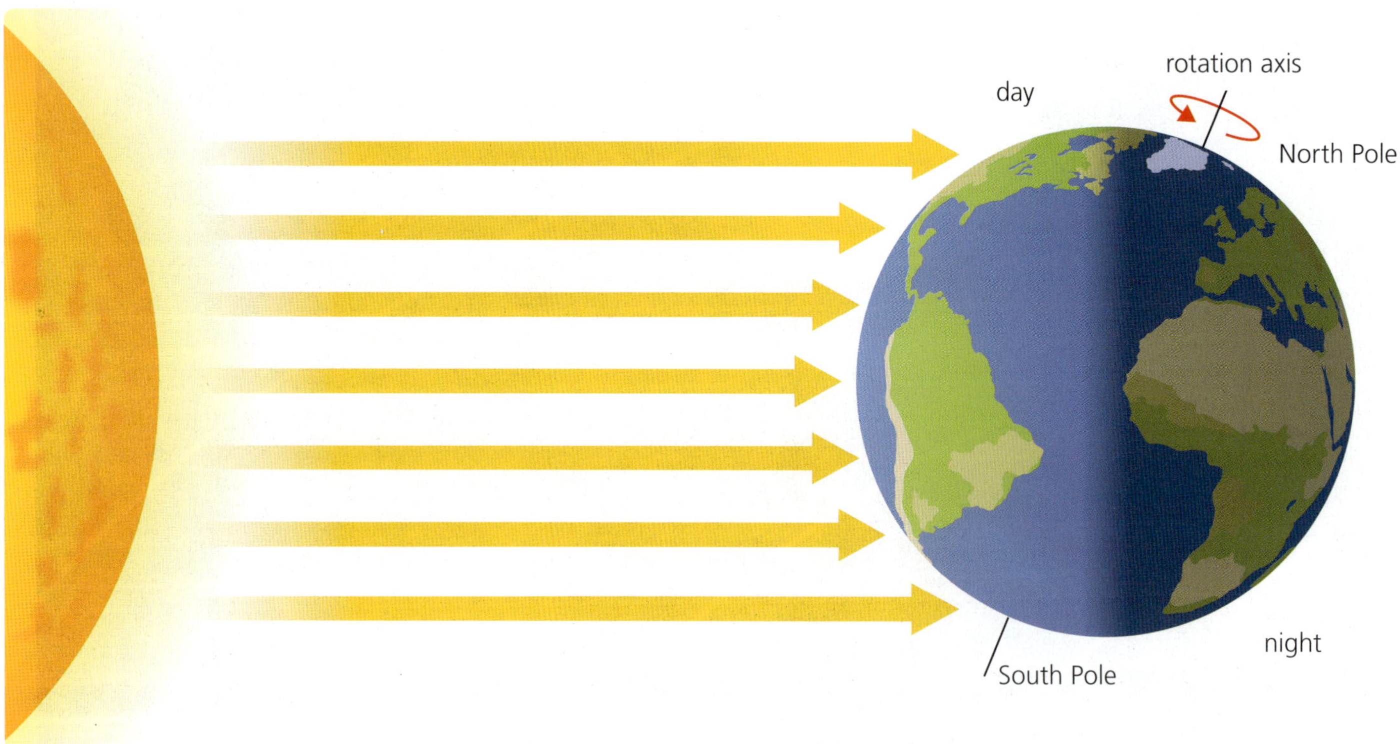

Day and night

Day and night vary in length according to the season and your distance from the Equator. At the Equator, day and night are approximately the same length all year round. As you get closer to the poles, winter nights become longer. Similarly, the closer you are to the pole, the longer summer days become. At the poles the effect is extreme. In summer you experience the **midnight sun**, while in winter the **polar night** lasts 24 hours!

The midnight sun

The polar night

The Earth's revolution

It takes the Earth just 365 days to orbit the Sun. During this period we experience different **seasons** because the Earth's axis is tilted. As a result, our part of the planet receives more or less light during different months. When the Northern Hemisphere is tilted towards the Sun, we receive more sunlight making it summer. During winter the opposite happens: the Earth is tilted away from the Sun and gets less sunlight. The first day of a season is called a **solstice** or an **equinox**. The solstices and equinoxes in the Northern Hemisphere are the opposite of those in the Southern Hemisphere.

The four seasons

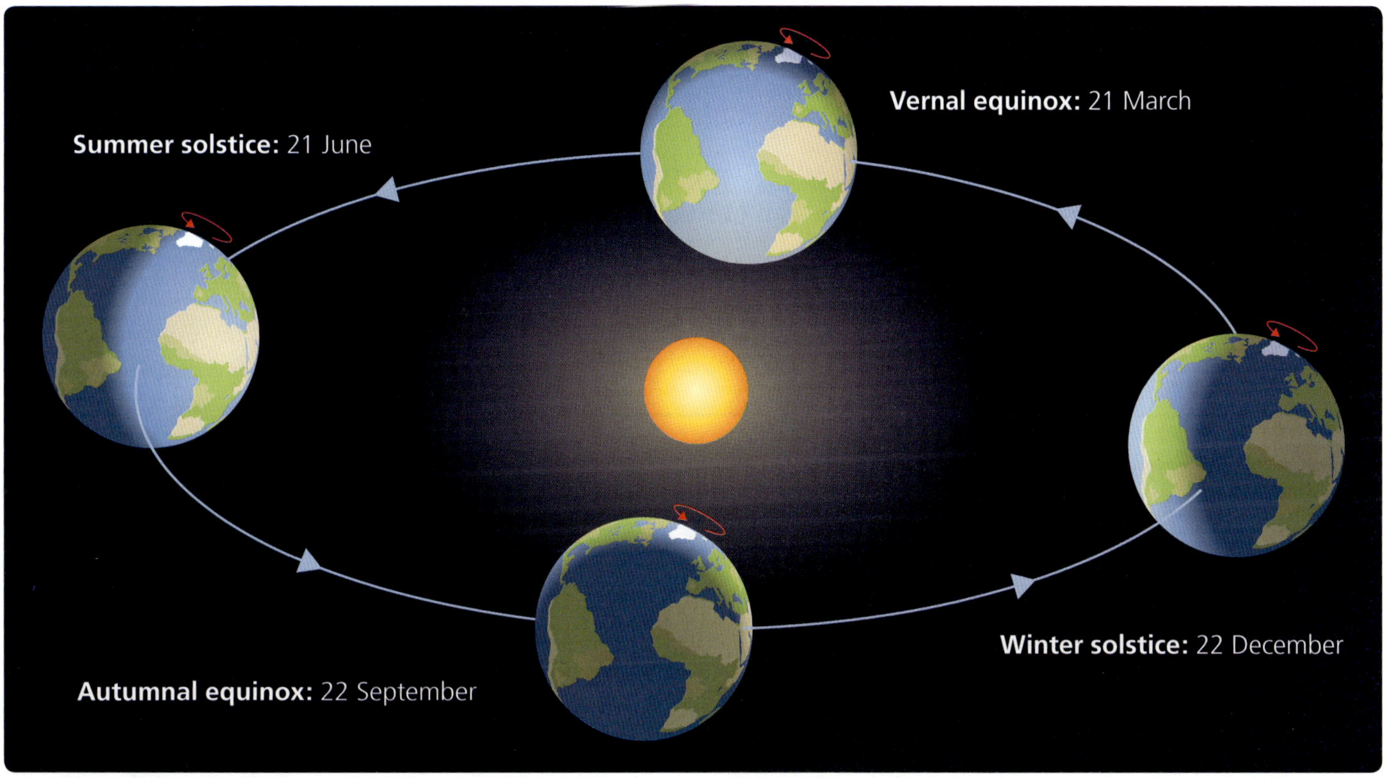

Equinoxes and solstices in the Northern Hemisphere

1. Why is it winter in the northern part of the world when it is summer in the southern part?
2. Explain the difference between the Earth's rotation and revolution. What does each of these types of motion cause?
3. What season is it in New Zealand now?
4. How do seasons affect life on Earth?
5. Do you think the seasons are the same all over the world? Why?

The Moon

What are artificial satellites?

The Moon is the Earth's only natural satellite and its nearest neighbour. It is about 384 000 kilometres from the Earth.

The **Moon** is around four times smaller than the Earth. It rotates on its axis and revolves around the Earth. It takes the Moon about **28 days** to complete one revolution and the same time to complete one rotation. This is why we always see the same side of the Moon from the Earth.

There is no air or atmosphere on the Moon because its gravity isn't strong enough. The temperature on the Moon varies from -153 °C at night to 123 °C during the day. The Moon's surface is rocky and has craters and mountains. These craters are caused when meteorites hit the surface of the Moon. We can observe these countless craters because the Moon has no atmosphere. There is also no wind or rain on the Moon to erode them.

The Moon doesn't produce its own light. We can see the Moon because it reflects sunlight. Obviously, we can only see the illuminated part that is facing the Earth. This is why, when we look at the Moon on different nights during the **lunar month**, its shape changes. These different shapes are called the **phases of the Moon**.

The near side of the Moon

The far side of the Moon

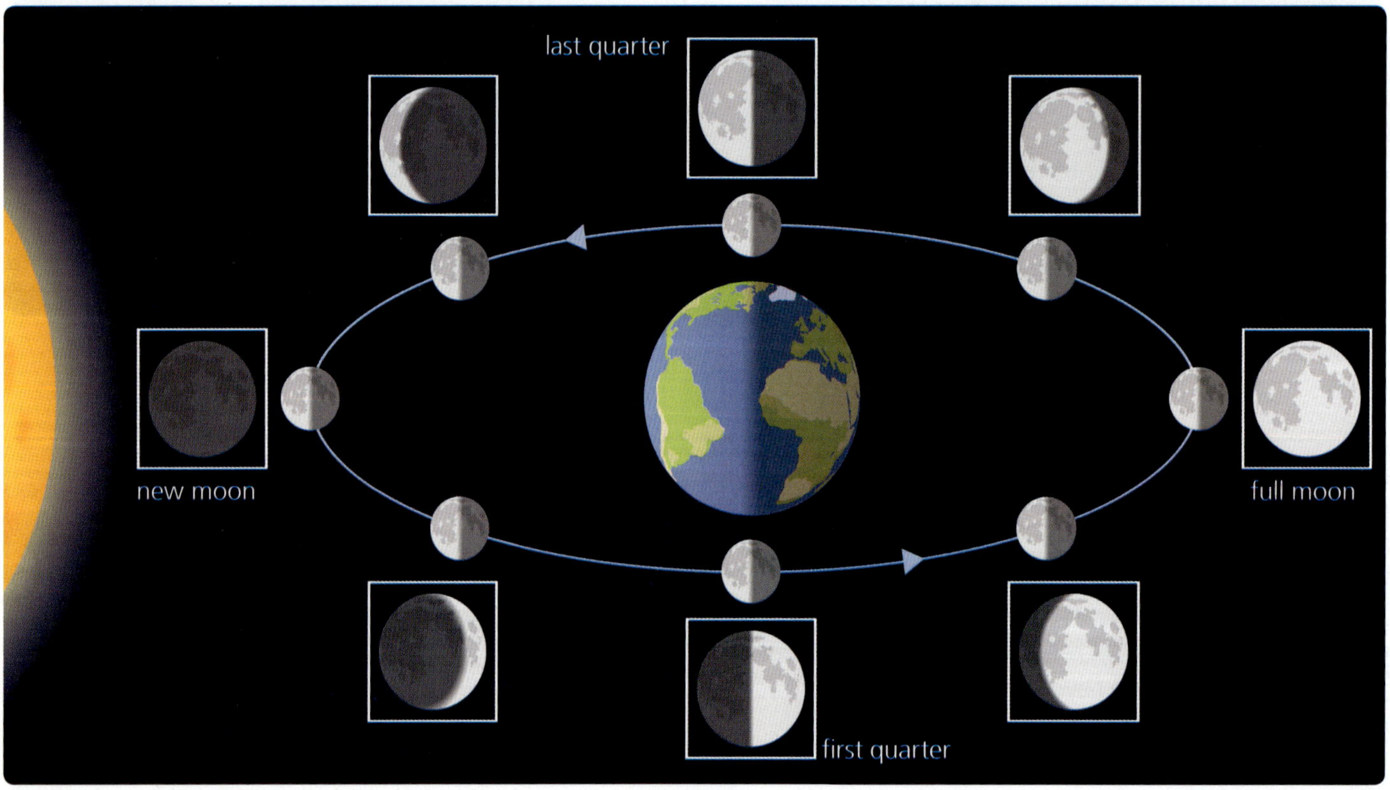

Phases of the Moon

Tides

Although the Moon is much smaller than the Earth, it has a great influence on our planet. The Moon's gravity pulls at the water in the oceans and creates tides. Tides are periodic changes in sea level. Every day we experience two **high tides** and two **low tides**.

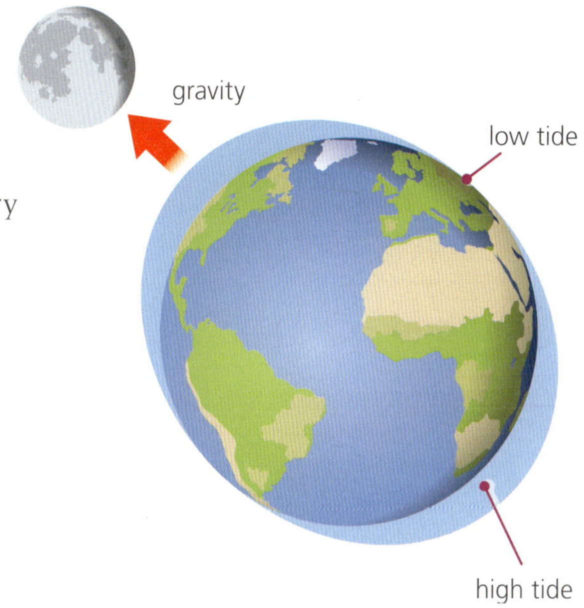

Eclipses

An eclipse occurs when a celestial body moves into the shadow of another. Eclipses can be solar or lunar:

- During a **solar eclipse**, the Moon blocks the sunlight and casts a shadow on the Earth.
- During a **lunar eclipse**, the Earth blocks the sunlight and casts a shadow on the Moon.

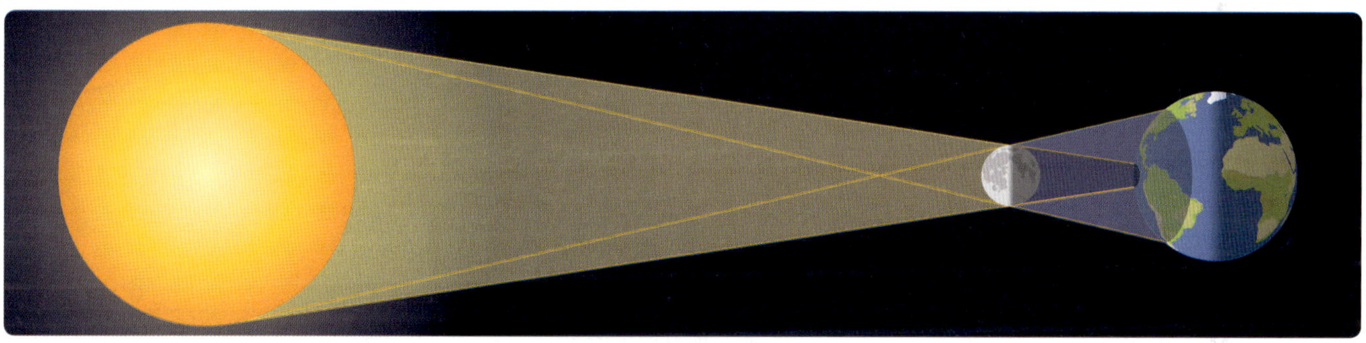

A solar eclipse

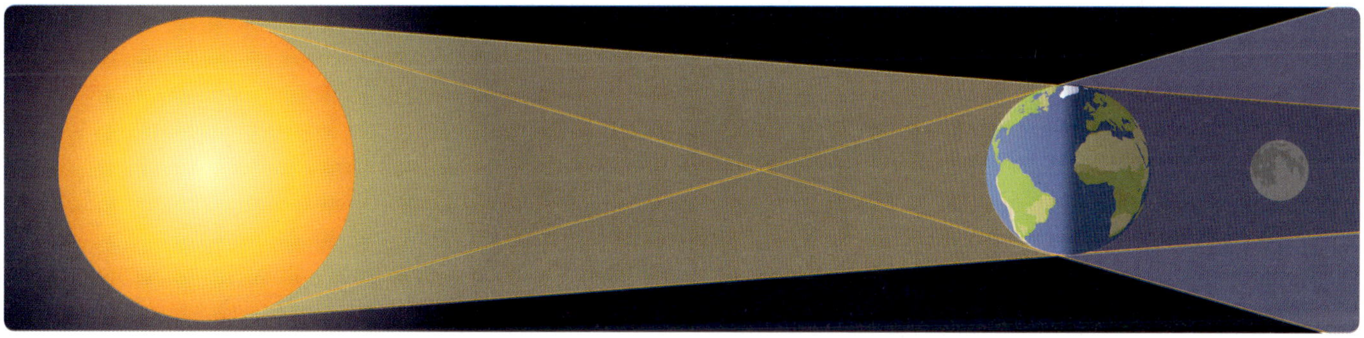

A lunar eclipse

1. What shape is the Moon? Why does it appear to change shape?
2. Can life exist on the Moon? Why?
3. What are the two types of motion of the Moon? Compare them with the motions of the Earth.

SCIENCE PROJECT: Build a planetarium

Aims

- Understand how a planetarium works.
- Learn about different constellations.

- a shoe box
- scissors
- printable constellation charts
- a pencil
- 4 pieces of card (9 cm × 8 cm)
- a torch
- a hole punch
- tape
- a few books
- a mat

Method

1. In one of the short sides of the box, cut a hole of about 8 cm × 7 cm.
2. Cut out a constellation from the constellation chart and place it over a piece of card. Poke holes through the dots with the punch.
3. Tape the card over the hole in the box.
4. Put a few books inside the box. Put the torch on the books. The torch should point to the corner of the box.
5. Darken the classroom and turn on the torch. Put the lid on the box. Project your constellations on the wall.
6. Repeat **steps 2** to **5** for several constellations.
7. Find some information about the constellations that you have chosen.

Conclusions

1. Which constellations did you choose? Find out more about them. Explain the origins of their names. Which is the brightest star in each of them?
2. Have you ever noticed that the night sky in winter looks different than in summer? We see different constellations at different times of the year. Why?
3. On a starry night, try to identify your constellations. Can you find all of them? Why?
4. Why don't we see stars during the day?

FRAGILE WORLD: Space debris

What is space debris?

Humans produce a huge amount of rubbish not only on Earth but also in space. Space debris (or space junk) is all the man-made material orbiting the Earth that is no longer used. It includes abandoned satellites, pieces of broken satellites, rocket parts and even human waste. There are more than 20 000 pieces of debris larger than a tennis ball orbiting the Earth. Millions of pieces are too small to be detected.

The problems with space debris

Space debris travels through space at a speed of about 27 000 kilometres per hour. At such a speed, even a very small object can damage a satellite or a spacecraft. When this happens, even more space junk is created. If debris enters the Earth's atmosphere, it usually burns up. However, occasionally larger pieces reach the Earth's surface. Scientists have proposed various solutions to remove space junk, but these continue to be expensive and require very advanced technology.

1. What is space debris? How does it differ from the rubbish that we produce every day?
2. List the problems that space junk creates.
3. Objects that are bigger than a tennis ball are tracked by radar. How can this be helpful?
4. How do think working satellites or spacecraft are protected from space junk?
5. Work with your friend. What could be done to reduce space debris? Think of some possible solutions.

Revise

Study skills

1 In your notebook, complete the diagram using the words in the box.

• asteroids • Pluto • comets • Saturn • Sun • inner planets

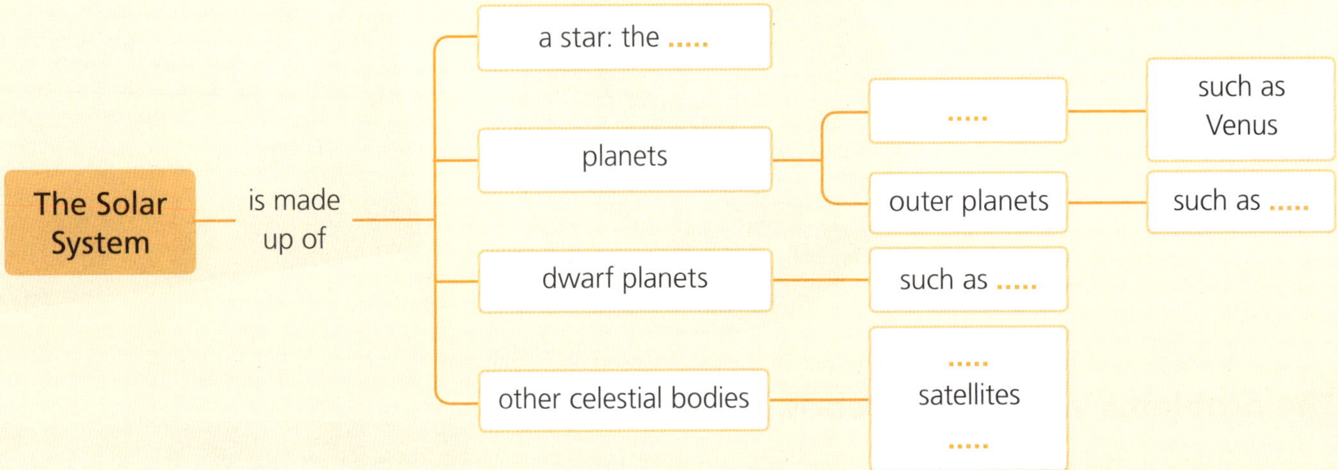

2 Read the text below (A). Then read the text about zodiac constellations (B) on page 150. In your notebook, decide whether the sentences below refer to text A, B or both.

A constellation is an artificial group of stars that appear to be close to each other when seen from Earth. They are, in reality, very far apart. The stars of a constellation form a pattern which depends on your point of view and your imagination. Throughout history constellations have been named after the mythological beings of different cultures. Greek astronomers named 48 of the 88 recognised constellations, such as the Great Bear and the Small Bear; Perseus, a famous Greek hero; and Pegasus, Perseus' mythological, winged horse. Many of these constellations were also recognised by the Arabs, Egyptians and the Babylonians. Modern astronomers have given names to the remaining constellations.

a. Stars in a constellation form patterns in the night sky.

b. Lots of the constellations' names have a Greek origin.

c. Pisces, Virgo and Capricorn are zodiac constellations.

d. There are 12 zodiac constellations.

e. Constellations are groups of stars which seem to be close to each other in the sky.

f. The constellation Pegasus is named after a horse with wings from Greek mythology.

Review

1 In your notebook, complete the sentences with the words from the box. There are some extra words.

constellation · inner · galaxy clusters · outer · geocentric · Milky Way · heliocentric · Kuiper Belt · dwarf

a. Galaxies group together forming .....
b. All the ..... planets have rings and moons.
c. The ..... model suggested that the Earth was at the centre of the Universe.
d. Mercury, Earth and Mars are ..... planets.
e. Pluto is classified as a ..... planet.
f. Our solar system is located in a galaxy called the .....

2 Name the celestial bodies in the photos and define them.

a

b

c
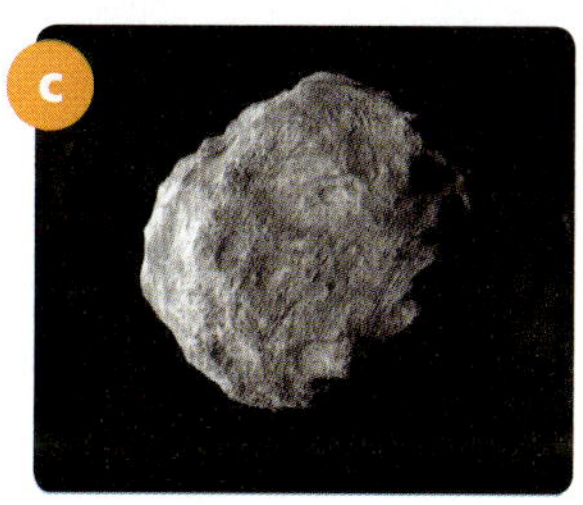

d

3 Explain the following phenomena. In your notebook, draw pictures.

a. solar eclipse
b. lunar eclipse
c. tide
d. phases of the Moon

4 In your notebook, complete the diagram using the words or phrases from the box.

day · winter · midnight sun · Northern Hemisphere · night · 365 days · equinox · rotation axis

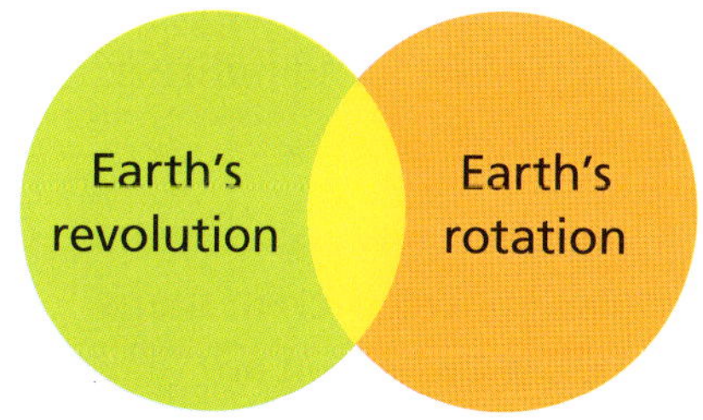

5 Talk about the Earth. Use the diagram to help you.

The Earth { rotates / revolves / belongs to / has } { one natural satellite. / on its axis. / around the Sun. / the Solar System. }

6 Complete the summary on page 151.

Checklist

- I can identify the different types of celestial bodies.
- I can explain where the Solar System is located in the Universe.
- I can remember what the Solar System is composed of.
- I can explain the motions of the Earth and their consequences.

2 Representing the Earth

① Read and discover.

The Earth consists of four components, or 'spheres', that work together as a complex system: water, air, land and life. These components interact and an event in one sphere can have both direct and indirect effects on other spheres.

We use maps and globes to represent what we know about the Earth. Different maps can provide us with information on landscapes, climate, countries or population. What instruments do scientists use to make maps?

2. Look at the large photo on page 22 and identify the four spheres of the Earth.

3. Each of the Earth's components interacts with each of the others. Think of some examples of this interaction. Use the words below as clues.
   - volcanoes
   - oceans
   - plants
   - oxygen
   - clouds
   - soil
   - rain
   - people

4. What are digital maps? How can they be useful?

5. Why are maps important? Imagine our lives without maps. Consider the following types of maps:
   - weather maps
   - road maps
   - city maps
   - political maps

Analyse and organise

① Maps use symbols to represent information. Look at the symbols and match them with their meaning in your notebook.

- train station
- museum
- toilets
- hotel
- bus stop
- car park
- hospital
- service station
- information centre
- restaurant
- post office
- shopping centre
- airport
- cycle lane
- castle/landmark
- telephone
- taxi stand
- school/university
- camping area
- place of worship

② Look at the map and identify the symbols from Activity 1. What is the shortest route from the information centre to the bus stop?

③ Read the text and decide if the sentences below are true or false.

Maps are drawings that use lines, symbols and colours to represent countries, landscapes and features, such as roads, parks and buildings. People have used maps for thousands of years. The oldest known maps were made in Mesopotamia around 2000 BC. These simple pictures were drawn on clay pots and showed very small pieces of land. Ancient maps were usually made by explorers and were not very accurate. There were no aeroplanes or satellites that could take photos of the entire Earth. As technology improved, maps became more accurate and detailed. The science of making maps is called **cartography**.

a. Maps are pictures of buildings.

b. The oldest maps are about 4000 years old.

c. Maps were always very accurate.

d. Modern maps are very detailed and accurate, thanks to scientific advances.

④ Look at the maps on the right and compare them with the modern world map.

⑤ Listen to the recording about the compass. In your notebook, complete the missing information.

- This is a device used for indicating .....
- The most common type of compass is a ..... compass.
- The main parts of a magnetic compass are the magnetised ..... and the diagram, called a compass .....
- The compass helps us identify the cardinal points easily: north, ..., east and .....
- The compass was probably invented by the .....
- Sailors started using the compass in the ..... century.

The spheres of the Earth

What do you think would happen if one of the spheres didn't exist?

The Earth is the only planet in the Solar System that can support life. The sphere of the planet where life exists is called the **biosphere**. The three spheres which support life on Earth are the **atmosphere**, the **hydrosphere** and the **geosphere**.

Atmosphere

The **atmosphere** is the layer of gases which surrounds the Earth. The atmosphere consists mostly of nitrogen, but it also contains oxygen, carbon dioxide and other gases which are essential for life on Earth. The atmosphere protects the Earth from harmful ultraviolet radiation, and helps maintain the Earth's temperature.

Biosphere

The **biosphere** is composed of all living organisms: animals, plants, fungi and microorganisms. It includes all the ecosystems on land and in the ocean and rivers.

Link it up

Does the Moon have an atmosphere?

Look at Unit 1.

Geosphere

The **geosphere** is the solid part of the Earth. It is made up of three layers: the **core**, the **mantle** and the **crust**.

- The **core** is the hottest part of the Earth. It's made of iron. The **outer core** is liquid metal. The **inner core** is solid because the pressure here is so strong that the iron solidifies.
- The **mantle** surrounds the core. Heat and pressure in the mantle can melt rock. This liquid rock is called **magma**.
- The **crust** is the outer layer of the geosphere. It's made up of **rocks** and **minerals**. The crust forms the continents, the islands and the ocean floors. The crust is thicker under the continents than under the oceans.

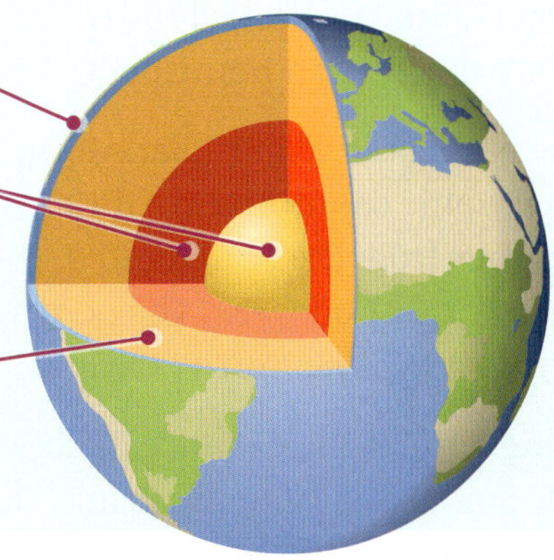

Hydrosphere

The **hydrosphere** is all the water that exists on Earth. Water covers about 75% of the planet. We can find water in all three states of matter: solid, liquid and gaseous.

1. Classify the words in the box according to the sphere they belong to.

   oceans oxygen core minerals animals

2. Explain the importance of the atmosphere.
3. Give two examples of water in each of the different states of matter.

In other words

The Earth is like an avocado:

- the crust = the skin
- the mantle = the flesh
- the core = the stone

Cartography

Find Spain, India and Brazil on a globe and on a map.

Geographic coordinates

To describe geographical locations on Earth, we use a system of imaginary lines called **parallels** and **meridians**.

- **Parallels** are circular lines that go around the Earth from east to west. The longest parallel, the **Equator**, divides the Earth into the Northern Hemisphere and the Southern Hemisphere.
- **Meridians** are circular lines that go from north to south and pass through the **poles**. Meridians are the same length. The **Prime Meridian**, also called the Greenwich Meridian, divides the Earth into the Eastern Hemisphere and the Western Hemisphere.

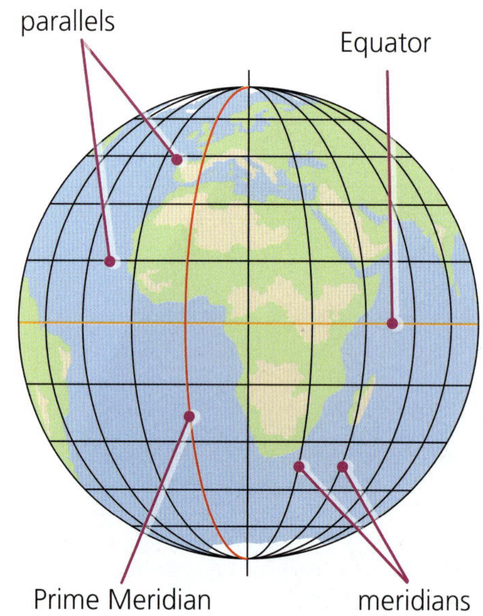

The parallels and meridians form a grid that we use to measure the geographic coordinates of different places. **Latitude** is the distance in **degrees** from the Equator (0°). The points north from the Equator are northern latitudes (**N**). The points south from the Equator are southern latitudes (**S**). The North Pole is at 90°N. The South Pole is at 90°S.

Longitude is the distance in degrees from the Prime Meridian (0°). The points east from the Prime Meridian are eastern longitudes (**E**). The points west from the Prime Meridian are western longitudes (**W**). The latitude of Madrid is 40°N. The longitude of Madrid is 3°W. The **geographic coordinates** of Madrid are 40°N, 3°W.

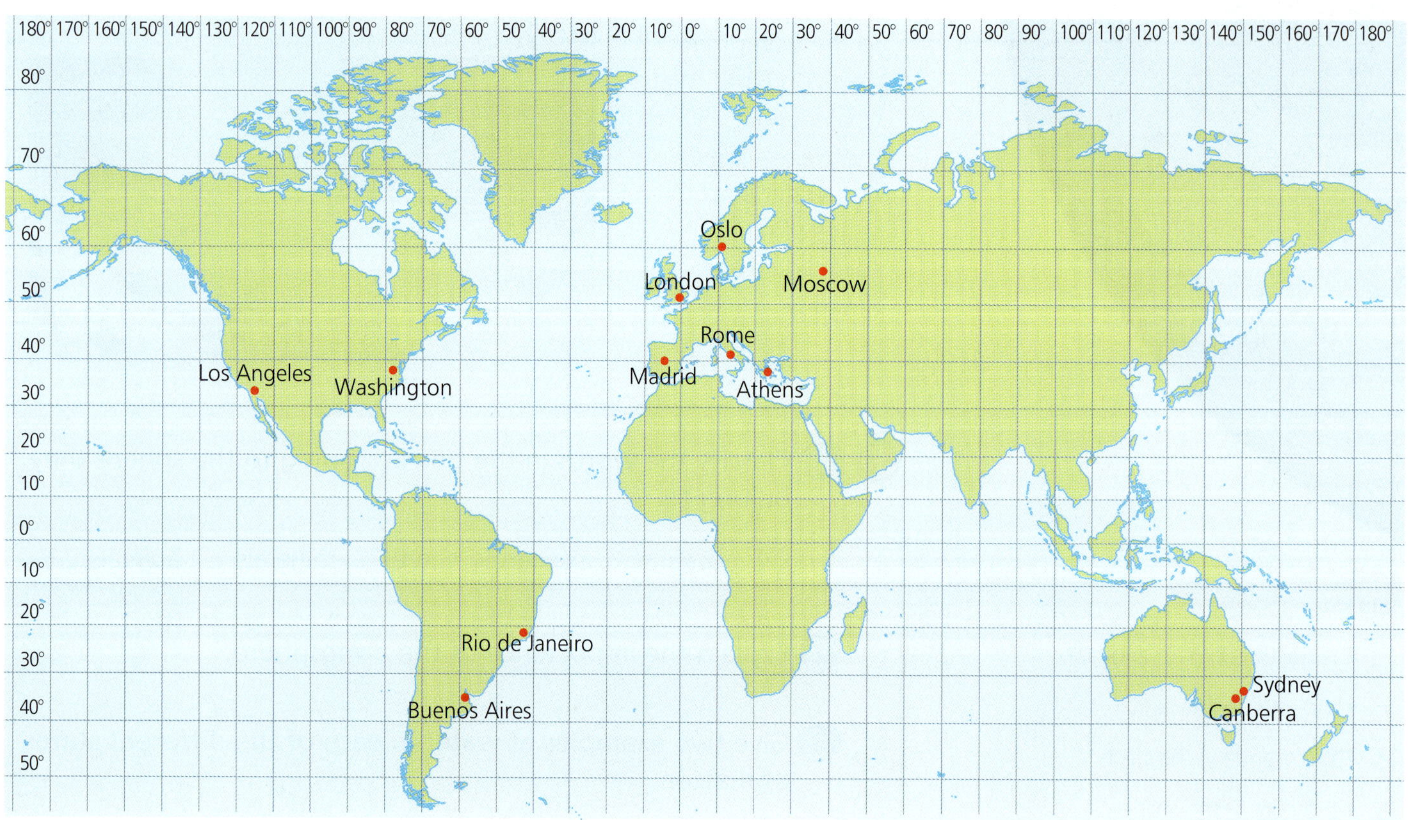

Characteristics of maps

- Features and objects on maps are represented using **symbols**. The meaning of these symbols is explained in a **key**.
- Maps include a **compass rose** that shows cardinal directions.
- Maps have a **scale**. A scale shows the relationship between the distances on the map and the actual distances on the Earth.

Did you know?

Map scales can be expressed in two ways:

- as a ratio (1:25 000) – every 1 cm on the map represents 25 000 cm in real life;
- as a graph 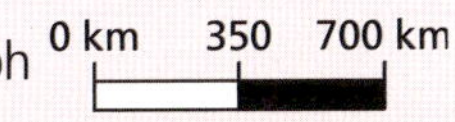

  – every 1 cm on the map represents 350 km in real life.

Political maps

Political maps show countries, their borders and capital cities.

1. Find and note down the geographic coordinates for Oslo, Canberra, Athens and Los Angeles.
2. Point to the countries that border Italy.
3. Identify the capital cities of Belarus, Iceland and Bulgaria.
4. Identify the key and the scale on the map above. What type of scale does this map use?

Landforms and weather

What types of maps do you know?

Physical maps

Physical maps show physical features, such as mountains, plains and rivers.

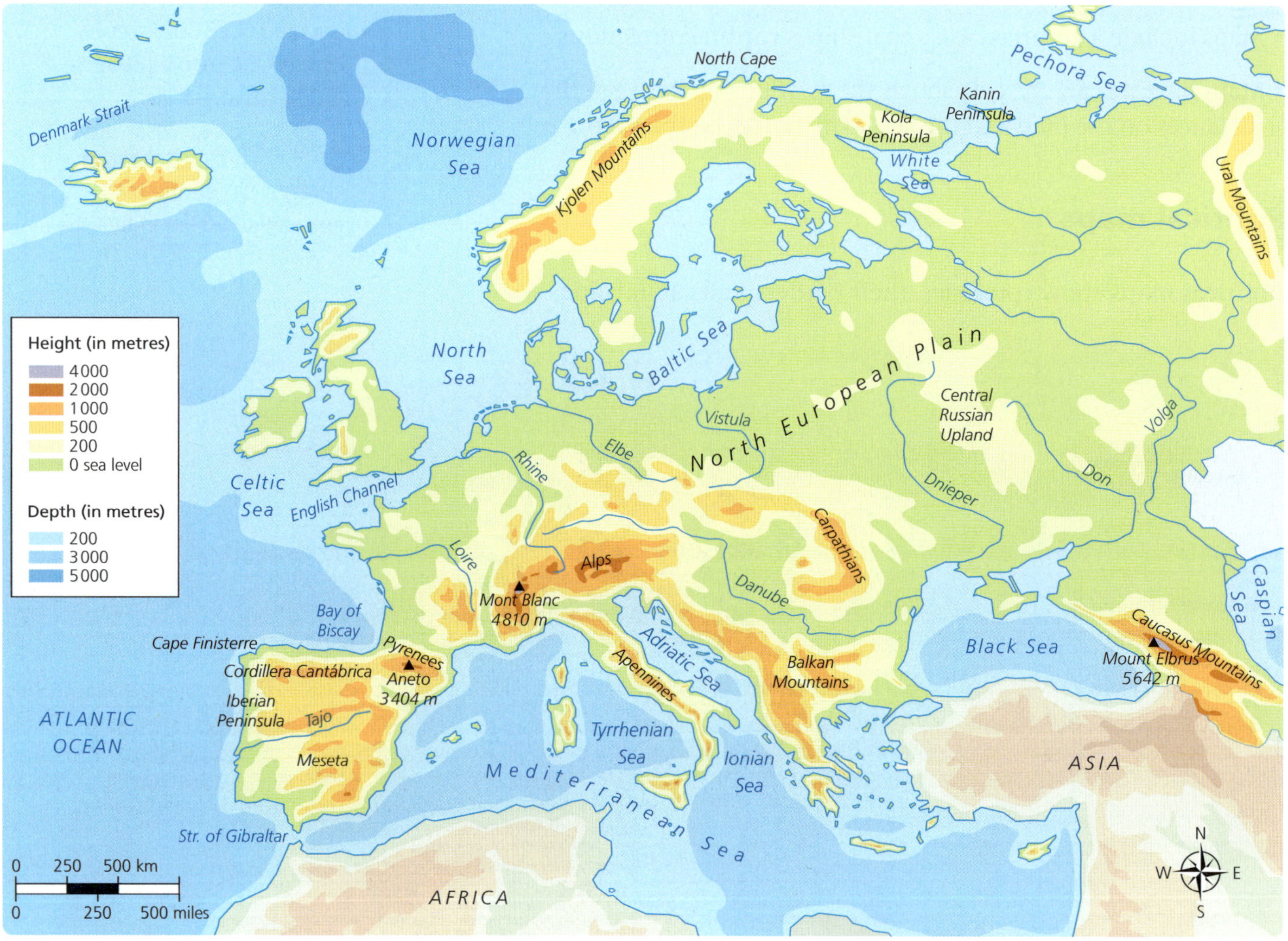

1. Identify the key and the scale on the map. What type of scale does this map use?
2. Identify the mountains in Europe. What countries do they run through? You can use the map on page 29 to help you.
3. Note down the countries that surround the Baltic Sea.
4. Note down the seas that border Greece.
5. Identify the rivers that flow through Germany.
6. Note down the countries that the Danube flows through.
7. Identify the highest peak in Europe.
8. Identify the main river in Spain.
9. Identify the highest peak in the Alps.

Weather maps

A **weather map** shows cloud cover, rainfall and temperatures.

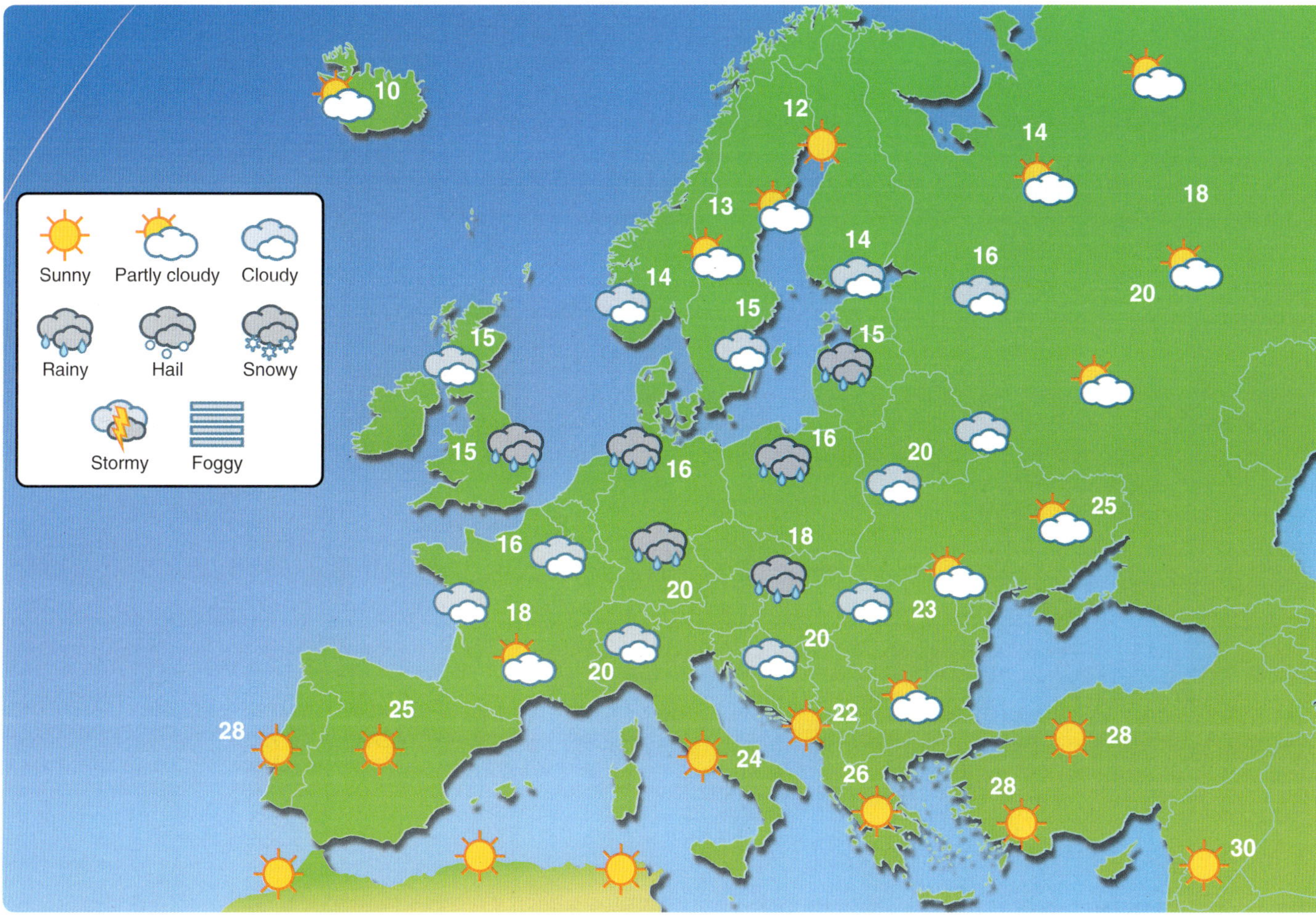

1. Look the weather map of Europe and answer the questions.
   a. What will the weather be like in London?
   b. Which country will have higher temperatures: Germany or Norway?
   c. Which country will have the highest temperature?

2. Look at the weather map of Spain. What will the weather be like in the following provinces: Málaga, Salamanca, Asturias, Alicante?

Globes and world maps

Look at the political world map. Which country is the biggest?

Globes are more accurate than maps for representing the Earth because they are three-dimensional like the Earth itself. Once you try to reproduce the surface of the Earth on a flat map, the sizes and shapes get distorted. Some countries appear larger than they really are.

A political world map

1. What is the biggest country in South America?
2. Identify the following countries and the continents they belong to:

   South Korea Ethiopia Colombia
   Estonia Venezuela Canada

3. Name the countries that share a border with:

   Mexico Argentina Algeria Mongolia Sweden

A political world globe

A physical world map

A physical world globe

1. What is the southernmost point of Africa called?
2. Identify the mountains that run through the United States and Canada.
3. What countries do the Andes run through? You can use the map on page 32 to help you.
4. What countries does the Sahara Desert cover?
5. What oceans border South America?
6. An atlas is a collection of maps. Explain why atlases are useful.

SCIENCE PROJECT: From A to B

Aim

Learn how to use a map and its scale to calculate distances.

Hypothesis

I think that using a piece of string to measure distance will be ...

- more efficient than using only a ruler, or
- less efficient than using only a ruler.

- a road map of Spain
- string
- a cup of water
- a felt-tip
- a ruler
- a calculator
- a pushpin
- a mat

Method

1. Wet the piece of string so that it sticks to the map.
2. Choose your starting point and destination.
3. Place one end of the string on your starting point and hold it with the pushpin. You can use a mat to protect your desk.
4. Place the string along the route from your departure point to your destination.
5. Make a mark on the string with the felt-tip, at your destination.
6. Measure the length indicated on the string with the ruler.
7. Calculate the distance by multiplying the length of the string by the ratio of the scale. For example, if the length indicated on the string is 10 cm and the scale tells us that 1 cm equals 20 km, the distance equals 10 × 20 which is 200 km.
8. Repeat the activity but use only the ruler to measure the distance between the two points. Which method is more accurate?

Test

- What type of scale does your map have?
- Is the route between the two points straight?
- Explain why we use string to measure the distance instead of using just the ruler.

Conclusions

1. How far is it from your departure point to your destination? Now check the distance given on the Internet or in an atlas.
2. If you were on a bus that travelled at 80 kilometres per hour, how long would the journey take?

Where are we?

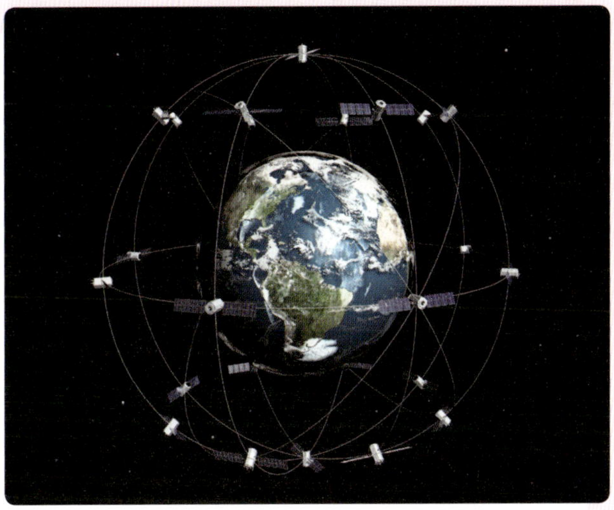

Did you know that there is a system that can find your exact location no matter where you are? It is called the **Global Positioning System** (**GPS**). Perhaps your parents have GPS in their car, but do you know how it works? GPS is a satellite-based navigation system that is able to create an exact view of the Earth; it uses 24 different satellites! The satellites send radio signals down to Earth. The signals contain information about the time the signal was sent. The information is then decoded and that time code is compared to the time kept in the GPS receivers. As long as the receiver is in contact with at least three satellites on the GPS network, a location can be found.

GPS can be green!

GPS technology, which was developed in the 1970s by the military, is now being used to protect the planet. It can help us understand and predict changes, such as volcanic or seismic activity. It can also help at times of ecological disasters. GPS receivers can track the movement of oil spills at sea and also map the spread of forest fires. Endangered animals can also benefit from this technology. By tagging animals with GPS tracking devices, experts can monitor and track animal populations and study their habits. GPS can even monitor animals during migrations and help in the fight against illegal hunting.

1. What is GPS? How does it work?
2. How can we use GPS in our daily lives?
3. Explain why the military developed this technology. What do they use it for?
4. How can GPS help the environment?
5. How do you think experts tag the animals they want to monitor?

Revise

Study skills

1 Complete the diagram with the information about the Earth.

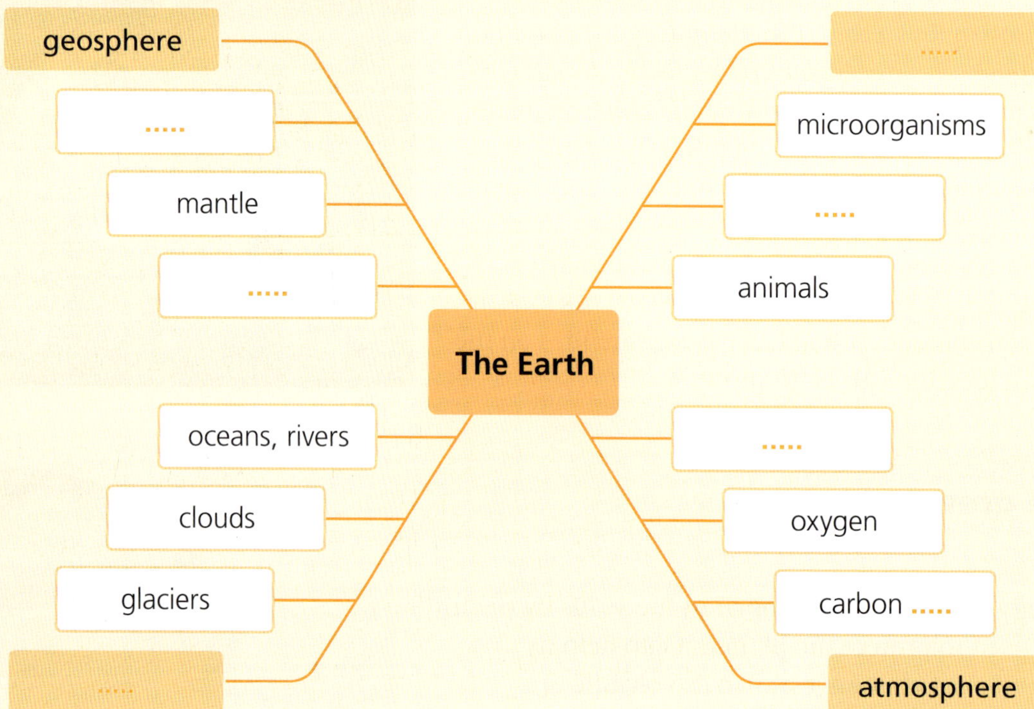

2 Look at the map below and the map and table on page 150. Answer the questions in your notebook.

a. What are some coastal tourist resorts in Andalucía?

b. Which Autonomous Communities have the highest average annual temperatures?

c. Which National Parks are located in the same Autonomous Community as Marbella?

d. Which Autonomous Community has more tourism: Región de Murcia or Cataluña?

e. Which Autonomous Communities have the lowest average annual temperatures?

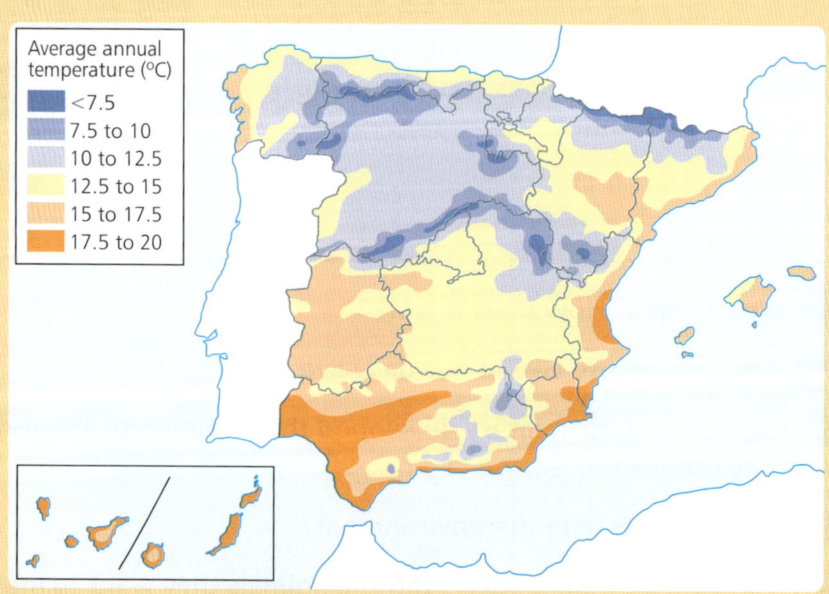

Review

1. Which type of map would you use to find the information below?

political map | climate map | road map | physical map

a. the capital city of Libya
b. mountain ranges in Asia
c. rivers in Europe
d. climate zones of the world
e. highways in Canada

2. Locate the following points on the map on page 28. Which countries are these cities located in?

a. 19 °N, 72 °E
b. 10 °N, 67 °W
c. 30 °N, 31 °E
d. 52 °N, 13 °E
e. 37 °N, 122 °W

3. In your notebook, match the numbers with the corresponding countries.

Sweden | Romania | Lithuania | Denmark | Greece | Slovakia

4. Decide if the following sentences are true or false.

a. The geosphere is composed of the core, the glaciers and the crust.
b. The Prime Meridian is at 0° latitude.
c. Globes are more accurate than maps.
d. The atmosphere protects the Earth from harmful gases, such as oxygen.

5. Talk about the spheres of the Earth. Use the diagram to help you.

The biosphere / The atmosphere / The geosphere / The hydrosphere

is composed of

the core / oxygen / living things / carbon dioxide / nitrogen / the mantle / the crust / the Earth's water in three states

6. Complete the summary on page 151.

Checklist

- I can identify the four spheres of the Earth and their characteristics.
- I can locate places on the Earth using geographical coordinates.
- I can interpret symbols and map scales.
- I can identify countries on a political map.

3 Climate and weather

① Read and discover.

Climate has a huge influence on our lives. It affects the food we eat, the energy we use, the work we do and the clothes we wear. Climate also influences the types of crops farmers cultivate and the kinds of houses people build. There are places that experience extreme weather conditions and, as a result, food and water resources are very limited. Think of some examples of extreme weather.

2 Look at the images and answer the questions.

- How do people adapt their houses to the climate?
- What clothes are most suitable for each of the places shown in the images?
- What do people in these places eat?
- How do they get water?
- How do they spend their free time?

3 Think of your own lifestyle and compare it with the lifestyles of people from the three images.

4 Think of plants and animals. How do they adapt to the conditions in different climate zones? Give some examples.

Analyse and organise

1 There are five elements of climate. In your notebook, complete the table using the words from the box. There are some extra words.

• ml • kilometres • mm • thermometer • vapour • scales

temperature	humidity	precipitation	wind	atmospheric pressure
• the amount of heat in the air • unit: degrees Celsius (°C) or degrees Fahrenheit (°F) • instrument:	• the amount of water ..... in the air • unit: percentage (%) • instrument: hygrometer	• water that falls from clouds • unit: millimetres (.....) • instrument: rain gauge	• the movement of air in the atmosphere • unit: ..... per hour (km/h) • instrument: anemometer	• the weight of the air in the atmosphere • unit: hectopascals (hPa) • instrument: barometer

2 Look at the pictures and identify the instruments from Activity 1.

a

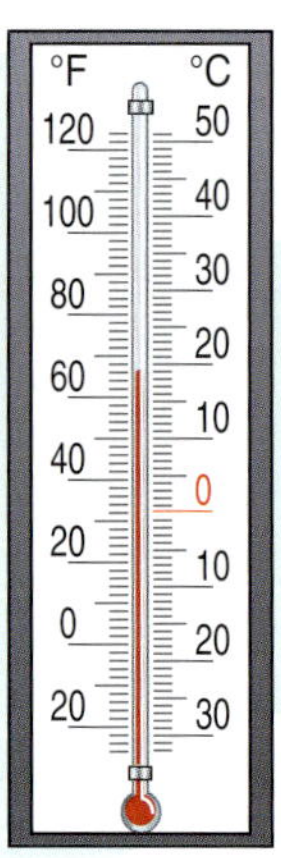

b

c

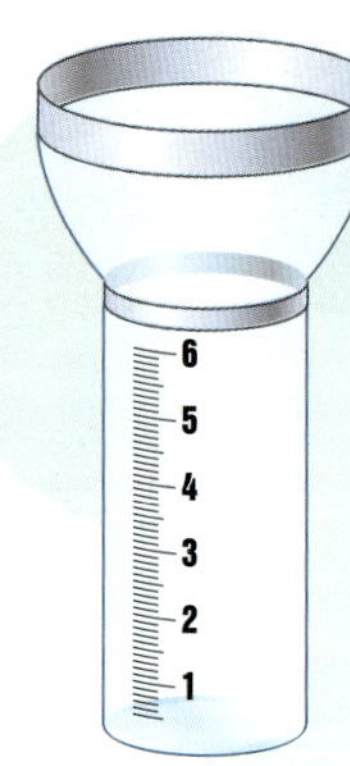

d

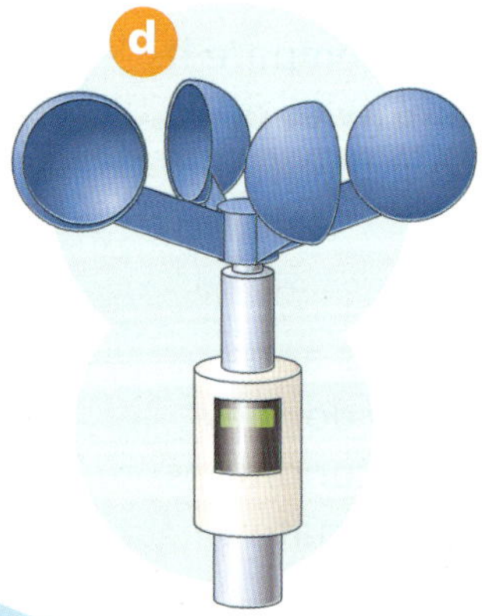

e

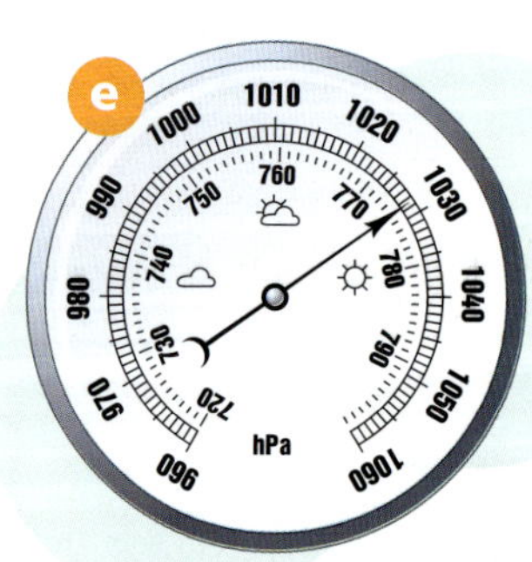

③ Read the text. Choose the best word for each space.

Scientists called (1) ..... are constantly observing and measuring the weather. They use special instruments to collect information and prepare weather forecasts. Predicting the weather not only helps us plan our daily (2) ....., but can also help prevent tragedies caused by natural disasters. Weather forecasts can predict floods, (3) ..... or tornadoes. Thanks to modern technologies which assist in predicting extreme weather, thousands of lives have been saved. People can be evacuated from their homes before disasters occur. Weather forecasts are also very important for (4) ..... who need to know weather conditions in order to transport passengers safely to their destinations. Weather predictions also help (5) ..... to know when to harvest their crops.

	a.	b.	c.
1	a. biologists	b. meteorologists	c. cartographers
2	a. activities	b. acts	c. exercises
3	a. earthquakes	b. storms	c. snow
4	a. taxi drivers	b. police officers	c. pilots
5	a. vets	b. farmers	c. doctors

④ Listen to the recording about instruments used for weather prediction. Complete the missing information in your notebook.

weather	This instrument records different types of information, such as ....., air pressure, humidity or wind speed.
..... map	This document shows different information, such as rainfall, minimum and maximum temperatures and cloud cover.
Doppler	This device can detect the intensity of precipitation and ..... speed and direction.

A Doppler radar

What affects climate?

Check the weather forecast. What will the weather be like tomorrow?

Weather and climate are two different things. **Weather** refers to the atmospheric conditions in a specific area at a specific time; sunshine, fog, precipitation, wind and atmospheric pressure. **Climate** refers to the average weather pattern in one place over a long period.

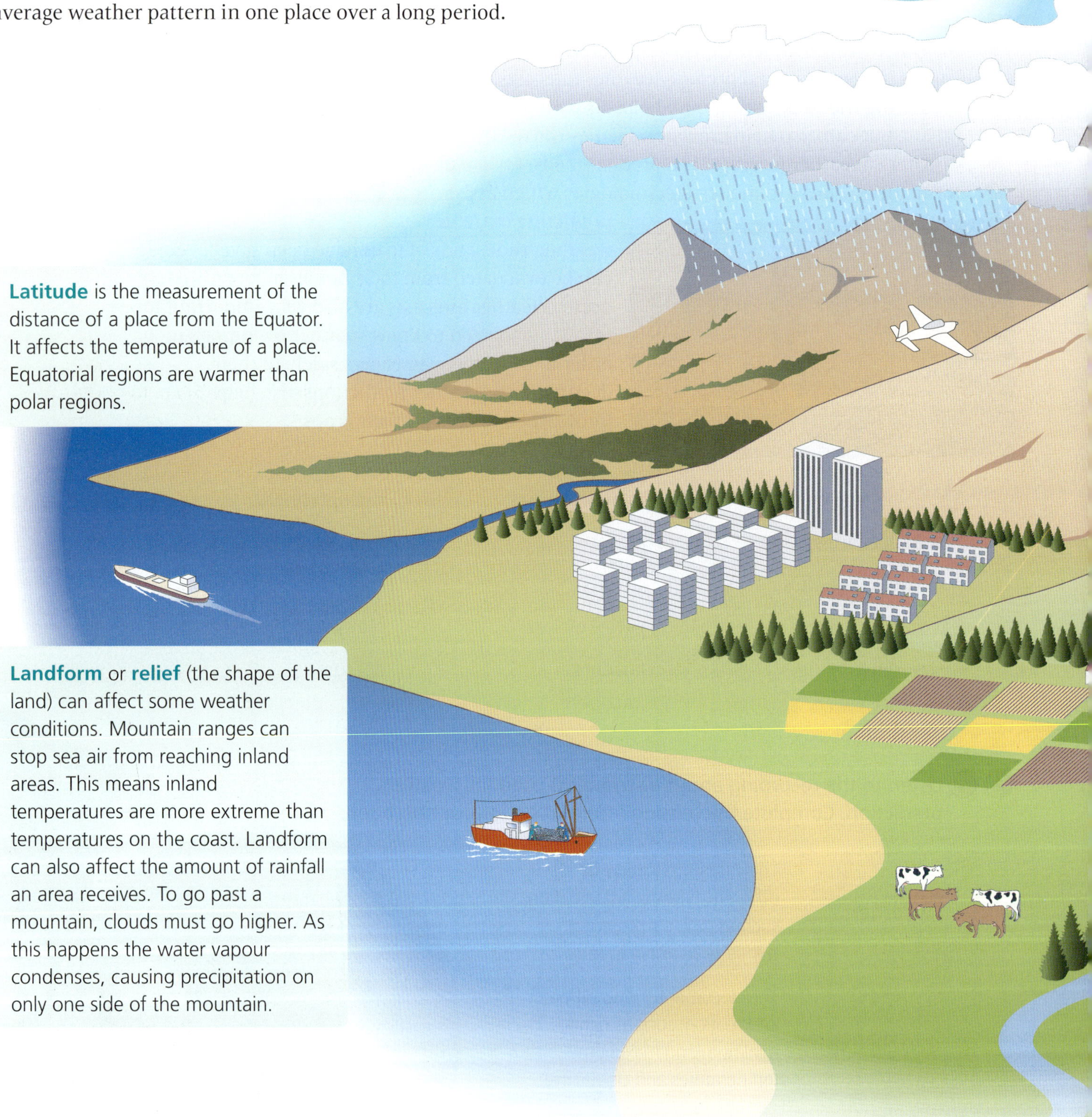

Latitude is the measurement of the distance of a place from the Equator. It affects the temperature of a place. Equatorial regions are warmer than polar regions.

Landform or **relief** (the shape of the land) can affect some weather conditions. Mountain ranges can stop sea air from reaching inland areas. This means inland temperatures are more extreme than temperatures on the coast. Landform can also affect the amount of rainfall an area receives. To go past a mountain, clouds must go higher. As this happens the water vapour condenses, causing precipitation on only one side of the mountain.

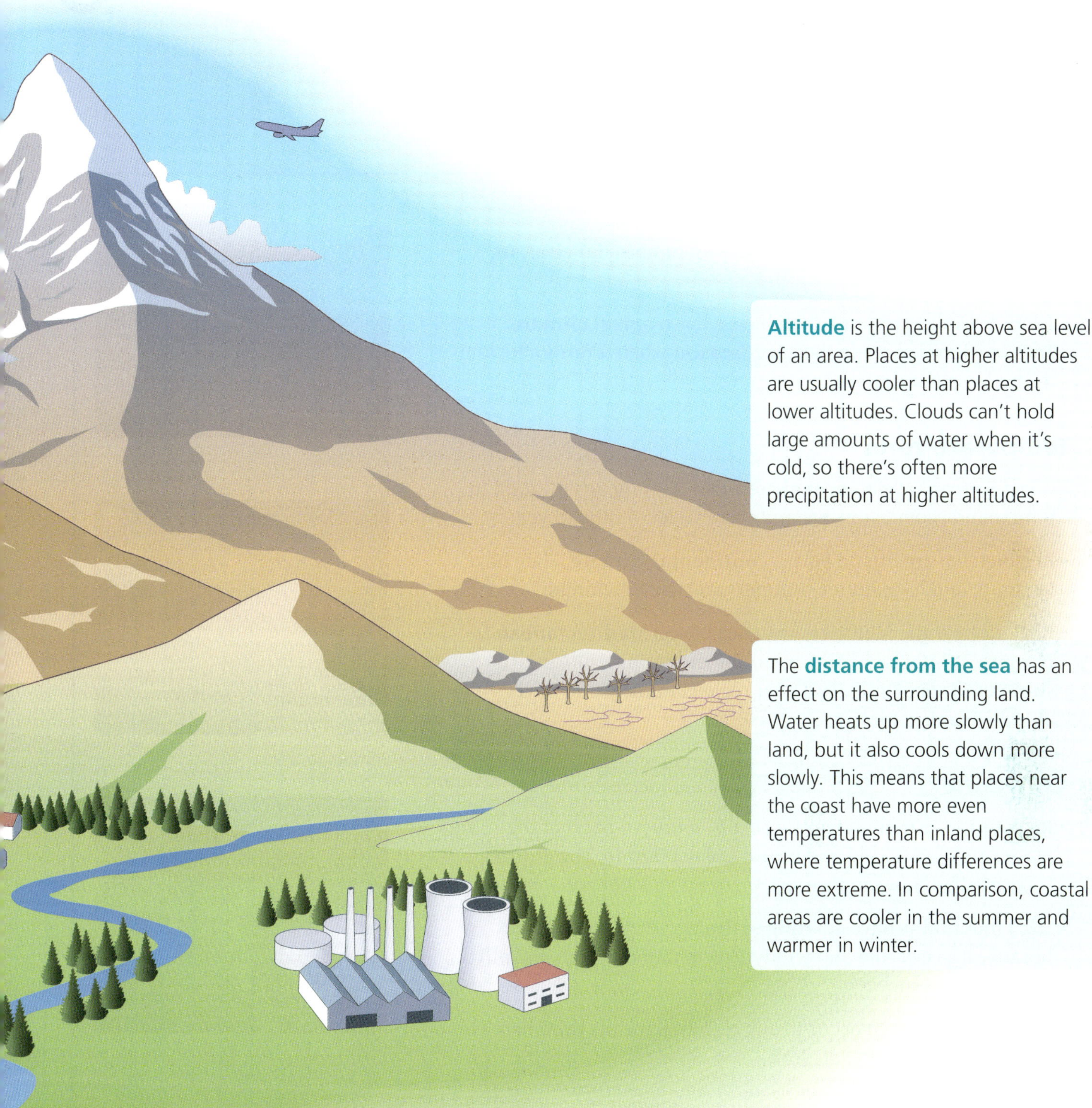

Altitude is the height above sea level of an area. Places at higher altitudes are usually cooler than places at lower altitudes. Clouds can't hold large amounts of water when it's cold, so there's often more precipitation at higher altitudes.

The **distance from the sea** has an effect on the surrounding land. Water heats up more slowly than land, but it also cools down more slowly. This means that places near the coast have more even temperatures than inland places, where temperature differences are more extreme. In comparison, coastal areas are cooler in the summer and warmer in winter.

1. Is altitude the same as relief? Explain why.
2. What are the four factors that affect climate? How do they affect climate? Identify which factors affect the climate where you live.
3. For each point decide which of the two cities has a warmer climate and say why.
   - Stockholm or Mexico City
   - Amsterdam or Moscow
   - Montreal or Barcelona
   - Sevilla or London

Climate zones

Which climate zone do you live in?

We can divide the Earth into three basic zones: **hot**, **temperate** and **cold**. There are several climates in each zone.

Hot zone

- Many regions near the Equator have an **equatorial climate**, which means it's hot and humid all year.
- There are some regions which have a hot **tropical climate**. These regions have one short **wet season** when it rains a lot and then a long, hot **dry season**.

Hot zone

Temperate zone

- Coastal areas have an **oceanic climate**. This means it's mild in winter and cool in summer and there's a lot of rain all year.
- Regions that are inland have a **continental climate**. They have less rain, and have hotter summers and colder winters.
- Regions near the Mediterranean Sea have a **Mediterranean climate**. Winters are mild, with a lot of precipitation and summers are hot and dry. Other regions in the world have climates similar to this.

Temperate zone

Cold zone

- Regions in the extreme northern and southern parts of the planet are always cold and have a **polar climate**. The ground is covered by snow and ice, but there isn't a lot of precipitation.
- High mountains have an **alpine climate**. There are no trees because it's very cold and windy. Precipitation is high, usually in the form of snow.

A **desert climate** can occur in any region. It means that there is little or no precipitation all year.

Cold zone

Did you know?

About 30% of the Earth's land surface is covered with deserts. The largest and the coldest desert is Antarctica. The average annual temperature in Antarctica is -57 °C.

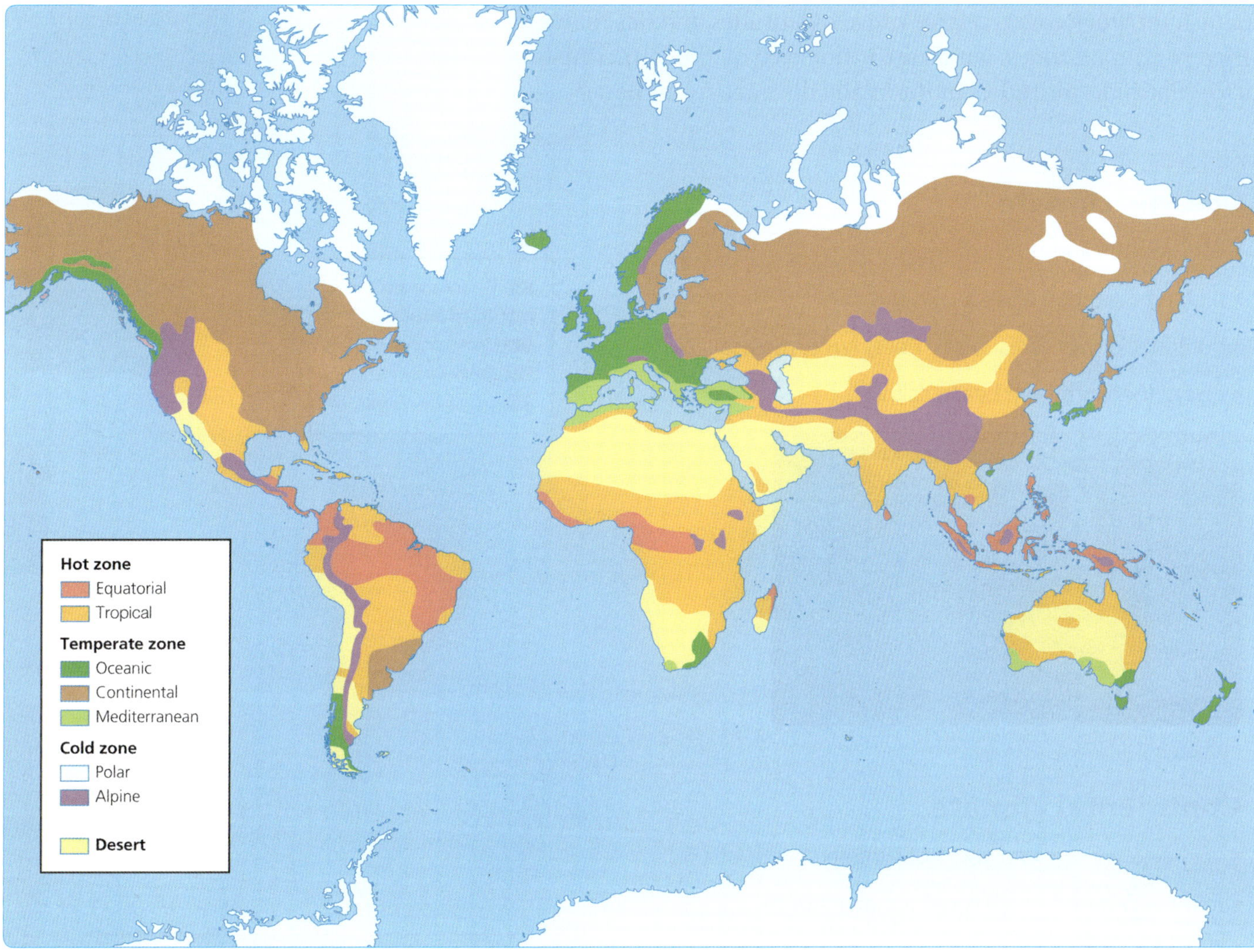

1. Look at the world map above. Write the names of two countries found in each of the climate zones.

2. What type of climate do these countries have? Some of them will have more than one.

- Canada
- Australia
- Morocco
- United Kingdom
- Brazil
- India

3. Look at the photos and identify the climates.

a 

b 

c 

d 

Climates in Spain

Look at the map. What is the main climate in Spain?

Spanish territory covers a large range of latitudes and has many different climate zones, which are influenced by the four climate factors: latitude, altitude, landform and distance from the sea.

Oceanic climate

- cool winters and mild summers
- high precipitation all year
- flora: deciduous forests, oak trees, ferns, mosses
- fauna: Iberian brown bears, salmon

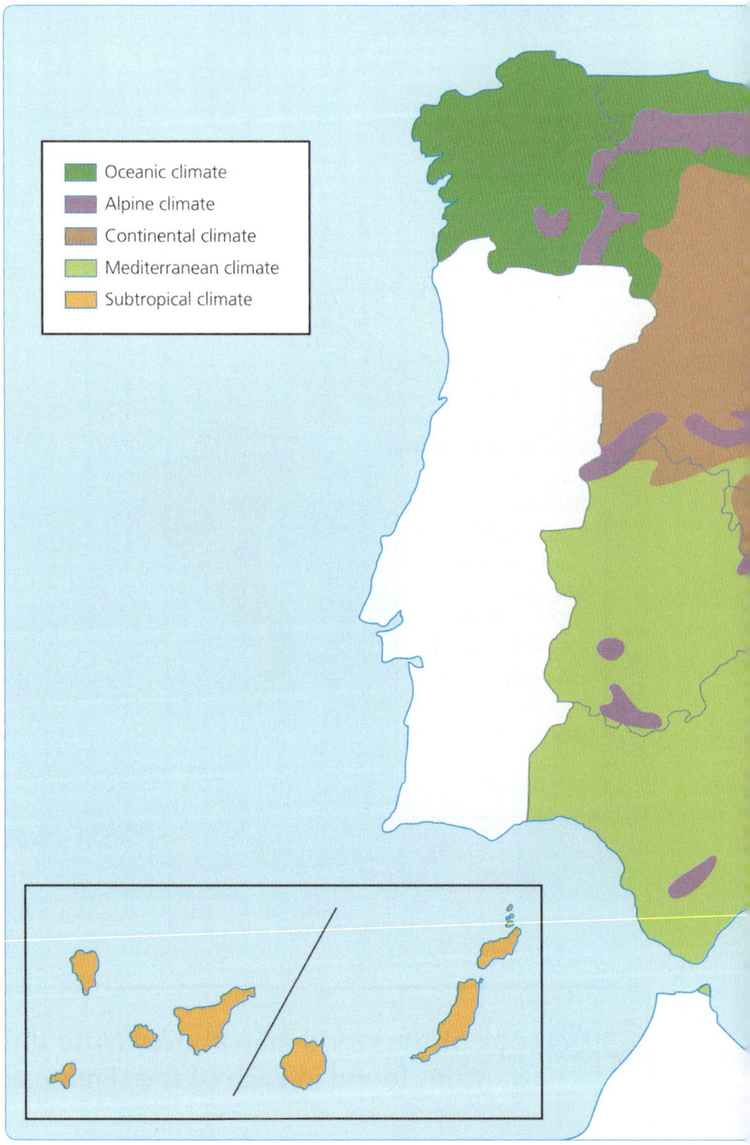

Continental climate

- very cold winters and very hot summers
- low precipitation, occasional summer storms
- flora: coniferous and deciduous trees, thyme
- fauna: deer, hares, wild boars, foxes, squirrels, trout

Subtropical climate

- mostly high temperatures all year
- low precipitation
- flora: pine trees, cacti, palm trees, dragon trees
- fauna: lizards, turtles

Link it up

What is cartography?

Look at Unit 2.

Alpine climate

- cold winters and cool summers
- high precipitation, often falling as snow in winter
- flora: oak trees and beeches at lower altitude, coniferous trees at higher altitude
- fauna: chamois, vultures, eagles

Mediterranean climate

- mild winters and hot summers
- low precipitation, but sometimes high in autumn
- flora: pine and oak trees, heather
- fauna: Iberian lynx, rabbits, flamingos

1. What type of climate do these places have?
   - Lugo
   - Alicante
   - Salamanca
   - Teruel
   - Tenerife
   - Oviedo
2. Describe the climate and the flora and fauna where you live.
3. Find out more about the climates in Spain. Add one plant and one animal to the list of characteristics of each climate.
4. Explain what these climates have in common:
   - continental and oceanic
   - subtropical and Mediterranean

SCIENCE PROJECT: Make a climate graph

Aim

Learn to make and interpret a climate graph. A climate graph shows average temperature and precipitation for an area. Climate graphs can be used to compare climates in different places.

- printable graphs
- printable charts
- a ruler
- a pencil
- red and blue pencils

Hypothesis

I think that average annual temperatures are higher in ...

- London, or
- New York.

Method

1. Use the photocopiable graph and chart with the information about the climate in London to make a climate graph.
2. Add the information about rainfall. Mark the average precipitation for each month by drawing a bar indicating the amount of millimetres listed in the chart.
3. Add the information about average maximum temperatures. Take a red pencil and mark the temperature by placing a dot over January. Do the same for each month.
4. Add the information about average minimum temperatures. Take a blue pencil and mark the temperature by placing a dot over January. Do the same for each month.
5. Connect the dots by drawing a line.
6. Follow **steps 2** to **5** to make the climate graph of New York.

Test

- What pattern do you see in the average monthly precipitation and temperature in both graphs?

Conclusions

1. Compare the two climate graphs. Were your hypotheses correct?
2. Which are the coldest months in New York?
3. Which are the wettest months in London?
4. Make a climate graph for a Spanish city. Compare your graph with London and New York.

What is global warming?

The Earth's temperature is increasing and the planet is getting warmer. As a result, glaciers around the world are melting. Scientists are worried because the increase in temperature is happening very quickly. This process is called **global warming**.

What causes global warming?

The main source of heat on the Earth is the Sun. Some of the gases in the Earth's atmosphere act like the glass in a greenhouse and stop some heat escaping back into space. That's why it's called the **greenhouse effect**! Without these greenhouse gases, heat would escape from Earth and the Earth's temperature would cool down. As the concentration of these gases increases, more heat becomes trapped and as a result the Earth's temperature increases. For this reason we should try to reduce the emission of greenhouse gases.

Carbon dioxide is the primary greenhouse gas which is emitted through human activity. Carbon dioxide is released when we burn oil, gas and coal for energy, and also through the petrol we use in cars. Petrol-based products which are often used in factories also produce carbon dioxide. These human activities on Earth increase the amount of greenhouse gases which are released into the atmosphere.

1. List some of the possible consequences of melting glaciers.
2. What is the greenhouse effect?
3. Why are high concentrations of carbon dioxide harmful?
4. Carbon dioxide can be beneficial too. Explain.
5. Work with your friend. Search for information about the Kyoto Protocol. Do you think this protocol is useful? Why?

Revise

Study skills

1. In your notebook, order the concepts using the table.

- Mediterranean climate
- cold
- polar climate
- temperate
- tropical climate
- continental climate
- alpine climate
- oceanic climate
- equatorial climate

climate zones		
hot	.....	.....
• ..... •	• ..... • ..... •	• ..... • ..... • alpine climate

2. Choose a climate from a hot climate zone. Find out about plants and animals that are characteristic of this climate.

3. Read the text about hurricanes (A). Then read the text about tornadoes (B) on page 150. In your notebook, decide if the sentences below refer to text A, B or both.

Hurricanes are formed in warm wet air masses above warm seas and oceans. They start off as normal storms, but as they absorb more heat and water, they become bigger and bigger. The difference in air pressure between warm air masses and the surrounding cool air causes the wind to move in spiral formations. Hurricanes bring very strong winds and heavy rain. Hurricanes can be up to 600 kilometres wide and can travel at up to 300 kilometres per hour! During a hurricane up to 25 centimetres of rain can fall in a single day.

a. They can travel at 500 kilometres per hour.
b. They form above warm oceans.
c. They are also called twisters.
d. They can cause enormous damage.
e. They bring heavy rains.
f. They can travel at 300 kilometres per hour.
g. Their centre is called a vortex.
h. They usually develop from storms.
i. They cause damage when the spinning vortex touches the ground.

Review

1 Read the sentences and decide which climate zones they refer to. Then, in your notebook, match the sentences with the corresponding climate zones.

a. This climate zone has cold winters and cool summers. The precipitation is high.

b. This climate zone has hot summers, mild winters and low precipitation.

c. This climate zone has high temperatures all year. The precipitation is low.

d. This climate zone has very hot summers and very cold winters.

e. This climate zone has high precipitation all year, cool winters and mild summers.

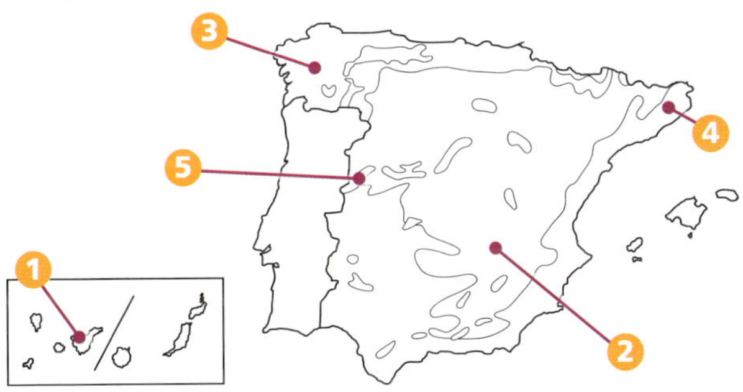

2 Which climate factor describes...

a. the distance from the Equator?

b. the height above sea level of a place?

c. coastal or inland areas?

d. shape of the land?

3 Search for information about average temperatures and precipitation in two Autonomous Communities. Draw climate graphs in your notebook and compare them.

4 Describe the climate in these cities.

a. Toronto

b. Benidorm

c. Buenos Aires

d. Cairo

5 Complete the table in your notebook.

	instrument	unit
temperature	......	......
precipitation	......	......
humidity	......	......
wind	......	......
atmospheric pressure	......	......

6 What will the weather be like tomorrow? Use the table to answer.

Tomorrow	it will it won't	be	sunny. rainy. windy. stormy. cloudy. foggy.

7 Complete the summary on page 151.

Checklist

- I can explain the difference between climate and weather.
- I can name the instruments used to measure the weather.
- I understand the five elements of climate.
- I can describe the climate in different areas in Spain.

TEAMWORK Climate change

1 Are these statements true or false? Correct the false ones in your notebook.

a. The Earth is getting warmer.

b. Human activity can increase global warming.

c. Greenhouse gases, such as carbon dioxide and oxygen, trap heat in the Earth's atmosphere.

d. Greenhouse gases are produced during the process of burning coal.

e. Sea level is rising because of melting glaciers.

2 Do any of these objects contribute to global warming? How?

3 Read and discuss. Justify your answers.

1 If temperatures keep rising, glaciers .....

a. will stop melting.

b. will start melting.

c. will continue melting.

2 If ..... continues rising, it will make more changes in our climate and our environment.

a. sunlight

b. rainfall

c. pollution

3 ..... trap heat in the atmosphere.

a. Raindrops

b. Greenhouse gases

c. Clouds

4 Greenhouse gases are produced during various types of everyday activities, such as .....

a. heating our homes and driving a car.

b. watching television and playing football.

c. swimming and growing crops.

The whole is greater than the sum of its parts.

Group project

4 Look at the photos. They show some of the consequences of climate change. How do they affect us?

a

b

c

d

5 In groups, make a climate change poster. In your poster you should include the following information:

- A definition or explanation of the following terms:
  - climate change
  - greenhouse effect
  - greenhouse gases
- Some of the effects of climate change, such as:
  - higher temperatures
  - more droughts
  - melting glaciers
  - changing rain patterns
  - rising sea level
- Different human activities that enhance climate change.
- Every little helps! What can we do to prevent climate change?

Use books or the Internet to look for pictures and extra information. Remember to include a reference list.

Checklist

- All group members contributed actively to the project.
- We generated ideas about how to prevent climate change.
- We explained some of the effects of climate change.
- We searched for new information from various sources.
- We illustrated the poster with pictures or diagrams.

Quick quiz

1. Listen to the quiz and choose the correct answer from the options.

	a.	b.	c.
1	a. planet	b. star	c. comet
2	a. seasons	b. tides	c. day and night
3	a. atmosphere	b. hydrosphere	c. biosphere
4	a. latitude	b. parallel	c. longitude
5	a. tropical	b. oceanic	c. continental
6	a. anemometer	b. hygrometer	c. barometer

2. Listen and check your answers.

A

B

C

D

Extended quiz

3. Read the quiz and write your ideas in your notebook.

1. What is another name for a meteor?
2. How long does a lunar month last?
3. What can you see in photos A–D?
4. What are the two types of climate in the cold zone?
5. What do we call a list of symbols used on a map with explanations of what they mean?
6. What is the geosphere made up of?

4. Listen to this student's answers. Match them to questions 1 to 6 in Activity 3.

5. Now listen to the answers in order. Check your original ideas from Activity 3.

Team test!

① Get into teams. Take turns to guess the words for definitions 1–9.

Team A

1 ..... : a huge explosion that most scientists believe created the Universe.
2 ..... : a small piece of rock or metal orbiting the Sun.
3 ..... : the biggest of the outer planets.
4 ..... : the outer layer of the geosphere.
5 ..... : a three-dimensional model of the Earth.
6 ..... : the longest parallel.
7 ..... : an instrument used for measuring the speed and force of wind.
8 ..... : the height above sea level.
9 ..... : the amount of water vapour in the air.
10 ..... : ________________.

Team B

1 ..... : one of the parts of a comet. It melts when it gets close to the Sun.
2 ..... : the inner planet located between the Earth and Jupiter.
3 ..... : a periodic change in sea level.
4 ..... : one of the Earth's spheres. It consists of various gases.
5 ..... : an instrument that shows direction.
6 ..... : the meridian that divides the Earth into the eastern and western hemispheres.
7 ..... : an instrument used for measuring atmospheric pressure.
8 ..... : another name for landform.
9 ..... : a unit used for measuring humidity.
10 ..... : ________________.

② Listen and check your answers.

③ Now, in your notebook, invent a tenth definition. Ask someone from the other team to guess the words for definitions 1–10.

4 Spain's politics and culture

① Read and discover.

Spain is a democratic country; democracy is a form of government where people elect their representatives. In 1978, the people of Spain voted for the Constitution. The constitution states the rights and obligations of citizens, as well as defending freedom, justice and equality.

Due to Spain's location, as well as its historical heritage, Spanish culture is considered to be both rich and diverse. How does a country's history influence its culture?

2. What are the key elements of democracy?
3. Do you know any other forms of government?
4. The word *democracy* has its origins in the Greek language. What does it mean?
5. What does the image above illustrate?
6. What festival is illustrated in the first image? Find out more about it. When and where does it take place?
7. Name other festivals that are held in Spain. When and where do they take place?
8. UNESCO World Heritage sites are places of a special cultural or physical significance. In Spain, there are 44 World Heritage sites. Find out more about them. Identify the one in the smaller image.

Analyse and organise

① Label the flags of the Autonomous Communities and autonomous cities in your notebook.

a. Castilla y León
b. País Vasco
c. La Rioja
d. Extremadura
e. Castilla-La Mancha
f. Ceuta
g. Islas Baleares
h. Principado de Asturias
i. Comunidad Foral de Navarra
j. Comunidad de Madrid
k. Cantabria
l. Comunidad Valenciana
m. Canarias
n. Galicia
o. Aragón
p. Región de Murcia
q. Andalucía
r. Cataluña
s. Melilla

② Find out about typical dishes from different regions of Spain. Then look at the map and compare the typical products from each of the different regions. What relationship can you see between the products and their locations?

③ Read the texts. Match the headings with the paragraphs. There are two extra headings.

Geography | Diversity | History | Languages | Gastronomy

1 Spain's unique culture is a result of its location, as well as the influence from different civilisations such as the Celts, Visigoths, Romans and Muslims. Spain's location has made it a natural bridge between the cultures of Europe, Asia, Africa and America. This cultural diversity has left its mark on art, festivals, languages and food.

2 Spain's official language is Spanish, also called Castilian. Spanish is not the only language spoken in Spain. Languages such as *català* (Catalan), *euskera* (Basque) and *galego* (Galician) have co-official status. There are also a number of unofficial languages or dialects that are spoken in certain places.

3 Spanish cuisine is extremely diverse and includes a variety of different ingredients and techniques. Spanish cuisine tends to make use of local fresh products. Each region has its own unique cuisine; however, there are some dishes which are considered national dishes such as *tortilla de patata* (Spanish omelette), *jamón ibérico* (cured ham) and *chorizo* (cured pork sausage) to name just a few.

④ Listen to the recording about the *Hogueras de San Juan* and, in your notebook, complete the table.

name	.....
date	.....
place	.....
patron saint	.....
celebrations	.....

⑤ Find out more about your region. Consider the languages spoken, food and festivals.

The Constitution

Who is the king of Spain? Who is his successor?

The **Constitution** is the most important law in Spain. It was approved on **6 December 1978**. The Constitution defines the organisation of Spanish territory, the organisation of the government and the rights and responsibilities of citizens.

The Constitution defines the flag, the national anthem and the coat of arms as the symbols of the State.

- The **flag** consists of three horizontal stripes: red, yellow and red.
- The **national anthem** is called the *Marcha Real* (Royal March) and it has no official lyrics.
- The **coat of arms** is made up of six other coats of arms, the Spanish national motto *Plus Ultra* (Further Beyond) and the Pillars of Hercules. This usually appears on the flag of Spain.

The flag of Spain

The coat of arms of Spain

Did you know?

The Pillars of Hercules are the huge rocks located where the Mediterranean Sea and the Atlantic Ocean meet. One of them is the Rock of Gibraltar and the other one probably Monte Hacho in Ceuta. They are named after the Roman hero called Hercules.

Find out about the myth of the Pillars of Hercules.

The Rock of Gibraltar

The Constitution establishes Spain as a **parliamentary monarchy**. This means that the king or queen is the Head of State but Parliament is responsible for making and approving new laws.

Felipe VI is the Head of State, but he doesn't establish laws. He represents Spain in international relations. He also holds the title of Commander-in-Chief of the Spanish Armed Forces. The Crown of Spain is hereditary.

Felipe VI

Leonor, Princess of Asturias

Rights and responsibilities of citizens

The Constitution defines rights and responsibilities that all Spanish citizens should respect.

Some rights

- We are all equal. Discrimination against anyone is forbidden.
- We have the right to be free and to be protected by the law.
- We have the right to use public services, including education and health services.
- We have the right to choose where we want to live and to travel freely.
- We have the right to a job.
- We have the right to vote and to elect leaders.

Some responsibilities

- We must pay taxes to pay for public services.
- We must protect the environment.
- We must respect the law.
- We must respect other people's beliefs, culture, language and religion.
- We must respect public services.
- We mustn't tolerate discrimination or unfair behaviour.

1. Find out more about the elements on the Spanish coat of arms. What does each element represent?
2. 'The Crown of Spain is hereditary'. What does it mean? Who is the heir to the Spanish throne?
3. On what occasions is the Spanish anthem played?
4. Analyse the lists of rights and responsibilities. Explain why they are important. Imagine what would happen if they didn't exist.

How is Spain organised?

Where are the main headquarters of the three powers located?

The Constitution establishes three powers: **legislative**, **executive** and **judicial**.

Legislative power

Parliament in Spain *(Las Cortes Generales)* is made up of two parts: the **Congress of Deputies** *(El Congreso de los Diputados)* and the **Senate** *(El Senado)*. Members of the Congress are called **deputies** and members of the senate are called **senators**. Both deputies and senators can make or develop laws, but the deputies can vote against a law developed by the senators. The main function of the senators is to represent the Autonomous Communities. Senators ensure that the Autonomous Communities follow the Constitution. Spanish citizens who are 18 years old or over vote for members of Parliament in **general elections** every four years.

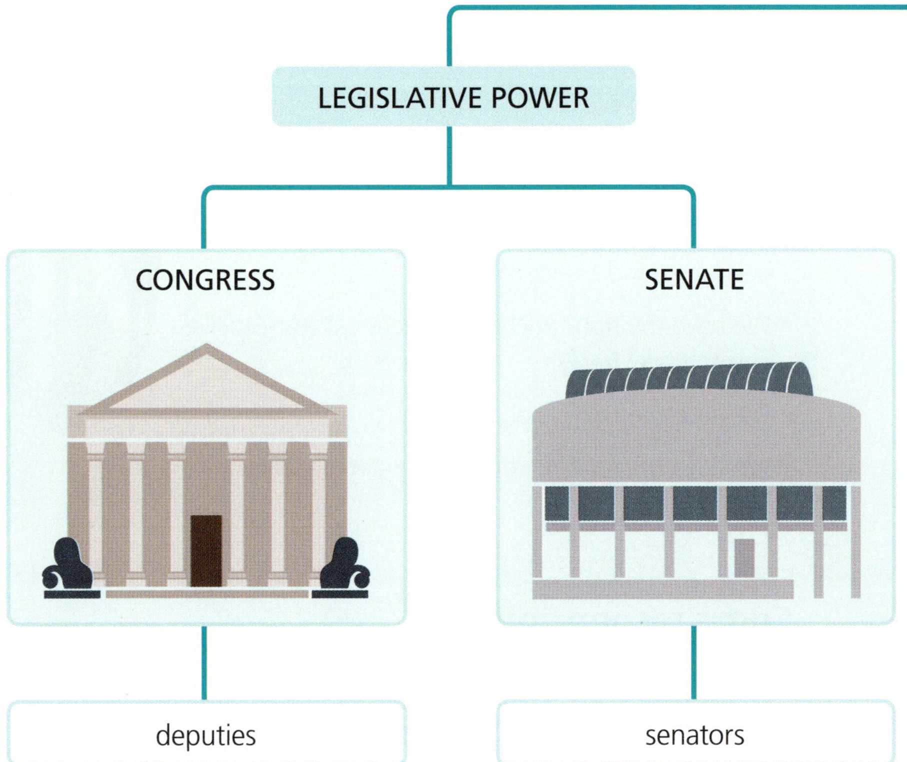

Executive power

Following the general elections, the party with the most votes forms the **Government** *(El Gobierno)*. The **Prime Minister** *(El Presidente del Gobierno)* is the head of the Government. The **ministers** are appointed by the Prime Minister. They work in different areas, such as education, healthcare, defence or the economy.

Judicial power

The judicial power in Spain belongs to **courts** and **tribunals**, composed of **judges** and **magistrates**. They ensure that the laws are obeyed. The highest judicial bodies in Spain are the **Supreme Court** *(El Tribunal Supremo)* and the **Constitutional Court** *(El Tribunal Constitucional)*.

- The **Supreme Court** is the highest court. It can accept or reject **sentences** passed in the lower courts.
- The **Constitutional Court** decides if laws introduced by Parliament are in accordance with the Constitution.

Did you know?

The Ombudsman of Spain *(Defensor del Pueblo)* is a public official appointed by Parliament whose job is to represent the interests and promote the rights of Spanish citizens.

THE CONSTITUTION

EXECUTIVE POWER

GOVERNMENT

Prime Minister

ministers

JUDICIAL POWER

SUPREME COURT

CONSTITUTIONAL COURT

judges and magistrates

1. Answer the questions in your notebook.
   a. Who is the head of the Government?
   b. Who chooses the ministers?
   c. Who represents the Autonomous Communities?
   d. Who develops laws?
   e. Who votes in general elections?

2. What do you think the Minister of Education is responsible for?

3. Find out more about the Spanish political institutions. Complete the sentences in your notebook.
   a. The Congress of Deputies has ..... members.
   b. The Senate has ..... members.
   c. The ..... and ..... are the major political parties in Spain.
   d. The ..... is the party governing Spain now.
   e. ..... is the Prime Minister.
   f. The ..... is now in opposition.
   g. ..... is the Leader of the Opposition.

Autonomous Communities

Look at the map. Which countries does Spain share its borders with?

Spain is divided into 17 **Autonomous Communities** and two **Autonomous Cities**: Ceuta and Melilla. Autonomous Communities are made up of one or more **provinces**, depending on the size of the Autonomous Community. Each province is then divided into **municipalities**.

The institutions

- The **Parliament** of the Autonomous Community is organised in the same way as the national Parliament. There are elections every four years. Citizens of the Autonomous Community who are 18 years old or over can vote for representatives. These representatives are called **deputies**. Parliament makes the laws and chooses the President of the Autonomous Community.
- The **President** represents the Autonomous Community and also names the **councillors** who are to make up the **regional government**. Each councillor has a specific responsibility, such as education or the environment.

The Statute of Autonomy

Each Autonomous Community has a **Statute of Autonomy**. Before the Statute can become law, the Spanish courts must approve it.

The Statute of Autonomy defines:

- the territory that forms the Autonomous Community;
- the capital city in the Autonomous Community;
- the official language or languages in the Autonomous Community;
- the government institutions in the Autonomous Community;
- the symbols for the Autonomous Community: its flag, its anthem and coat of arms;
- the legal power in the Autonomous Community.

Issues concerning local services, such as town planning, culture and sports, can be decided by the autonomous government. The national government is responsible for wider issues, such as justice.

Link it up

What climate zone is your Autonomous Community located in?

Look at Unit 3.

1. What is more important: the Constitution or the Statute of Autonomy?
2. Which Autonomous Communities are made up of only one province?
3. Name the provinces in your Autonomous Community.
4. Who is the President of your Autonomous Community?
5. Find out about the population in your Autonomous Community. Is it high or low?
6. Calculate the population density in your Autonomous Community. What information do you need to do it?
7. Find out more about the Statute of Autonomy in your community. What type of information does it include?

SCIENCE PROJECT: Class elections

Aims

- Recognise the importance of voting within a democracy.
- Decide which issues are most important to students in the class.

- a large piece of card
- coloured pencils
- felt-tips
- scissors
- a glue stick

Hypothesis

I think that students in the class ...

- can contribute to making the classroom a better place, or
- can't contribute to making the classroom a better place.

I think that good ideas ...

- will attract votes, or
- won't attract votes.

Method

1. Get into groups of four or five. Ensure that your group has the following members:
   - a candidate
   - secretaries
   - poster designers
2. Prepare the campaign.
   a. Decide on changes you want to introduce in the classroom.
   b. Choose a message.
   c. Create your campaign poster.
   d. Prepare a speech.
3. The candidate should present the project to the class outlining the roles of the different members of the group.
4. The class votes for the best project.

Conclusions

① Did everybody in the class vote?

② Was there a clear winner? Did everyone in the class respect the result?

③ What had most influence on the voting: the message, the speech or the poster?

④ Do you think that a good campaign could win more votes than an important message?

Democracy in Spain

In a democratic society, citizens choose their representatives by voting in an **election**. In Spain, there are national and municipal elections every four years.

Before the elections, political parties run a **campaign**. In a campaign, the candidates explain their ideas for improving society. They also explain their plans and ideas in a document called a **manifesto**.

On Election Day, citizens vote by choosing a piece of paper with the name of the political party and the list of candidates they want to support. Each paper is sealed in an envelope and placed in a **ballot box**. The voters choose the deputies (or councillors for local elections) who then choose the Prime Minister (or mayor for local elections).

The importance of elections

Elections are very important because they allow people to express their opinions and to help make important decisions in society. Every citizen has the responsibility to vote in democratic elections.

- Voting is the most important right citizens have.
- In many places in the world, people do not have the right to vote.
- By voting, people can make sure that their opinions are heard.
- In most countries, you can exercise your right to vote when you're 18 years old or over.

1. How do Spanish citizens participate in the political process?
2. Explain what a manifesto is.
3. Why should citizens participate in elections?
4. What happens when people do not have the right to vote?
5. Why are political campaigns important?

Revise

Study skills

1 Use the words in the box to complete the diagram in your notebook. There are some extra words.

- deputies
- ministers
- Autonomous
- judicial
- Court
- Supreme
- Constitution
- Parliament
- legislative
- Government
- Senate
- province

- **Three powers**
  - .....
    - .....
      - Congress — .....
      - ..... — senators
  - executive
    - .....
      - Prime Minister
      - .....
  - .....
    - Constitutional .....
    - ..... Court

2 Read the text about the festival of Sant Jordi (A). Then read the text about the festival of San Isidro (B) on page 152. Copy the table into your notebook and complete the information about the festivals.

One of the most famous festivals in Cataluña is the *Diada de Sant Jordi* which is celebrated on 23 April. Sant Jordi (Saint George) is the patron saint of soldiers and also of Cataluña. According to legend, he rescued a princess from a terrible dragon. When Sant Jordi killed the dragon, a red rose grew from the animal's blood and he gave this rose to the princess. This rose became a symbol of love and friendship. Nowadays, on 23 April the streets of Catalan towns and villages are full of stalls where people can buy books and flowers. People celebrate the day by walking in the streets and buying a rose and a book for their family and friends.

	A	B
name	.....	.....
date	23 April	.....
place	.....	.....
patron saint	.....	.....
celebrations	.....	.....

Review

1. Label the map in your notebook. Write the name of the capital city and the provinces of each Autonomous Community.

2. Complete the table in your notebook. Then explain why these institutions are important. What would happen if they disappeared?

Head of State	Parliament
Name:	Members: .....
Responsibilities:	Responsibilities: .....

Government	Courts of Justice
Members:	Members: .....
Responsibilities:	Responsibilities: .....

3. Explain the following terms.

   a. *Marcha Real*
   b. *Plus Ultra*
   c. Constitution
   d. Congress

4. Collect information about your Autonomous Community. Then write a short text using the information you have found. Consider the following:

   a. capital city
   b. provinces
   c. population
   d. climate
   e. landforms
   f. landmarks
   g. food
   h. festivals

5. Choose another Autonomous Community that interests you and use the instructions from Activity 4 to write a text about it.

6. Talk about citizens' rights and responsibilities. Use the diagram to help you.

We	can should must mustn't	be good citizens. obey the law. tolerate crimes. travel freely.

7. Complete the summary on page 153.

Checklist

- I can explain the division of power in Spain.
- I can identify the main political institutions in Spain and their functions.
- I can explain the territorial organisation of Spain.
- I understand the importance of the Constitution.

5 Spanish population

① Read and discover.

The Spanish population increased significantly during the 20th century. This was primarily due to the promotion and improvement of sanitation and also due to an increase in immigration. Spain has a population of 46 million, five million of whom are immigrants. Have there been any changes in migratory movements in Spain recently?

2 Look at the images on both pages. Compare Spanish society in the past with the present.

3 What do you think is meant by the expression 'an economically active population'? Who belongs to this group? Who doesn't belong to this group?

4 How have living conditions in Spain changed since the beginning of the 20th century?

5 Why do people migrate?

6 What is the difference between an immigrant and an emigrant?

7 Do you think migratory movements are always positive? Why?

8 What are the differences between life in villages and cities?

Analyse and organise

1. There are different ways to classify population. In your notebook, complete the diagram using the words from the box. There are some extra words.

• location	• city	• girl	• adult	• urban

Population

- age
  - child
  - .....
  - elderly
- .....
  - rural
  - .....
- economic activity
  - active
  - inactive

2. Classify people in the photos according to the population group. Some of the people may belong to more than one group.

a

b

c

d

e

f

③ Read the text and decide if the sentences below are true or false.

We can classify populations as urban or rural according to the number of inhabitants. A population of 10 000 or more is considered urban, while anything below that is classified as rural. Urban populations are located in large towns or cities, where people usually work in industry or provide a service. Rural populations, on the other hand, are located in villages, and people usually work in agriculture. One hundred years ago, most inhabitants in Spain lived in rural areas. Today, most Spaniards form part of the urban areas.

a. Population can be classified according to the number of economically active people.

b. People in cities usually work in factories and provide services.

c. There are more people living in rural areas now than 100 years ago.

d. An urban population has more than 10 000 inhabitants, who usually work in industry.

e. Most Spaniards work in agriculture.

④ Listen to the recording about the advantages and disadvantages of living in the city. Complete the missing information in your notebook.

advantages	• more ..... opportunities (companies) • more opportunities to study (schools, ...) • better healthcare (....., ambulances) • many ways of spending free time (museums, ..., cinemas, parks)
disadvantages	• ..... cost of living • high population density (cars, traffic ....., noise) • more pollution • sometimes ..... to find open spaces for sport and games

⑤ Add one advantage and one disadvantage to the table.

Our changing population

The **absolute population** of an area is the number of inhabitants in that area. The absolute population is constantly changing. We can understand the changes in a population by looking at the birth rates and death rates and immigration and emigration statistics. The science that studies these characteristics is called **demography**.

Natural increase

We call the difference between the number of births and the number of deaths **natural increase**.

- A **positive** natural increase means the birth rate is higher than the death rate. The absolute population **increases**.
- A **negative** natural increase means the death rate is higher than the birth rate. The absolute population **decreases**.

natural increase = birth rate – death rate

Actual increase

To find out the **actual increase** of a population, we add the number of immigrants to the natural increase and then subtract the number of emigrants. The actual increase can also be **positive** or **negative**.

actual increase = natural increase + number of immigrants – number of emigrants

There are many causes of migratory movements:

- natural causes, such as floods, earthquakes and droughts;
- social causes, such as wars, hunger and poverty;
- economic causes, such as job opportunities.

Population density

Population density shows us how populated an area is. We calculate population density by dividing the number of inhabitants by the size of the area they live in. The measurement for area is square kilometres (km^2).

$$\textbf{population density} = \frac{\text{population}}{\text{square kilometres}}$$

Identify the different population groups in the picture.

In other words

There are over 7 billion people in the world and this number is constantly growing. In one year about 130 million babies are born and about 55 million people die. This means that the global population grows by about 75 million a year. This number is comparable to the combined populations of Spain, Greece and the Netherlands.

1. Look at the information below. Did the actual population increase or decrease?
   - births = 930
   - deaths = 490
   - immigrants = 357
   - emigrants = 96
2. What is the population density of a region if 3 000 000 people live there and the region has a surface area of 600 000 km^2?
3. What is overpopulation? List some of its possible consequences.
4. Decide if the causes of migration listed below are economic, social or natural.
   - earthquake
   - hurricane
   - unemployment
   - political problems
   - drought
   - war
5. A census is a survey of all the people in the country. It's organised every 10 years. When did the most recent census of the Spanish population take place? Why is a census important?

Characteristics of the Spanish population

Why has the Spanish population increased so much since 1900?

The Spanish population increased steadily during the 20th century. In 1900, there were approximately 18 million inhabitants in Spain. Today, Spain's population is about 46 million.

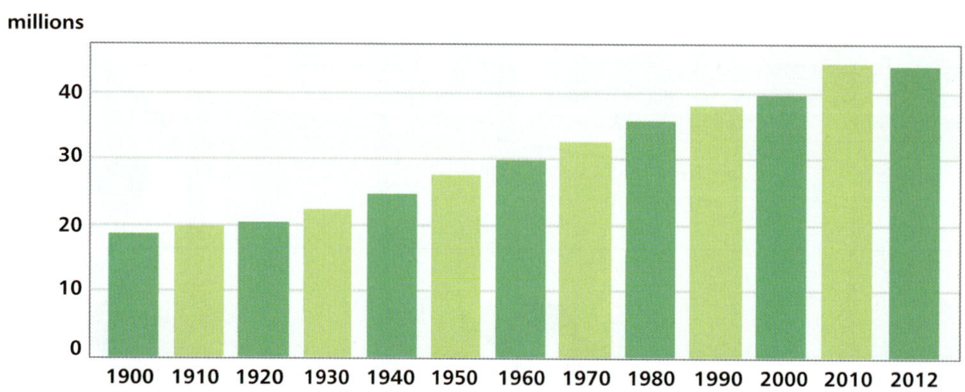

Positive natural increase

Although the birth rate hasn't increased, the death rate has experienced a decrease. Like other European countries, Spain has more elderly people than ever before. Medical care and hygiene have improved and nutritious food is more widely available. There's a better quality of life, which means people are living longer.

Positive actual increase

Many more people come to Spain than leave it. There are now over five million immigrants living in Spain. Many left their countries because of natural disasters or social problems. Most come to Spain looking for work and a better life for themselves and their families.

Life expectancy

Life expectancy is the average number of years that people live. In 1900, life expectancy in Spain was 35 years. Now it is about **81 years**, although this varies for men and women.

Number of children per woman

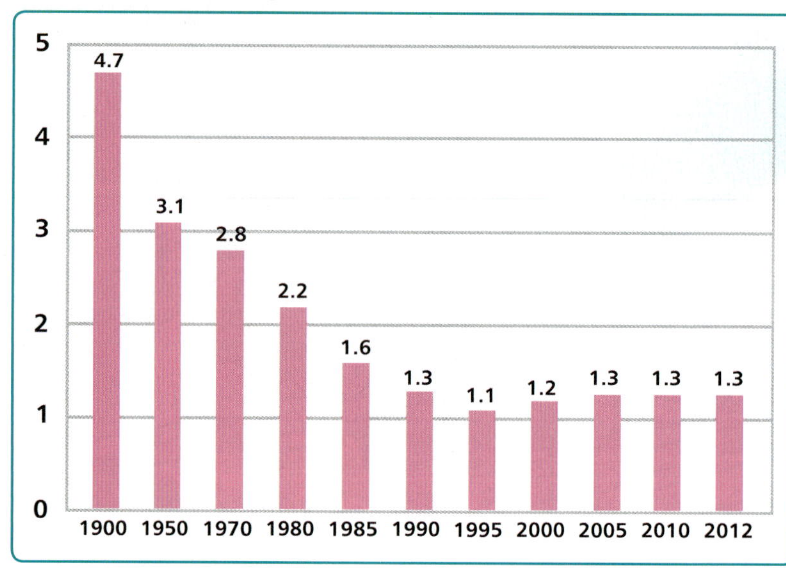

Life expectancy by sex

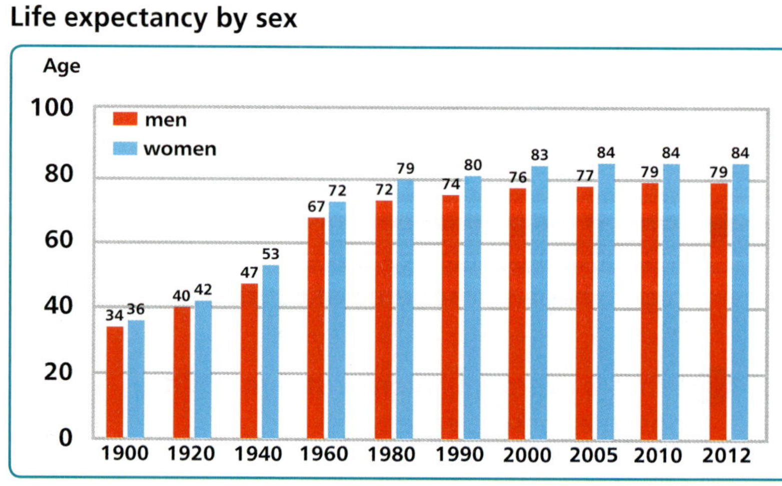

The distribution of the Spanish population

Spain has a population density of **93 inhabitants per square kilometre**. This is low compared to other European countries. Spain's population is mostly **urban**. About 78% of Spanish inhabitants live in urban areas. The most densely populated areas in Spain are large cities and coastal regions.

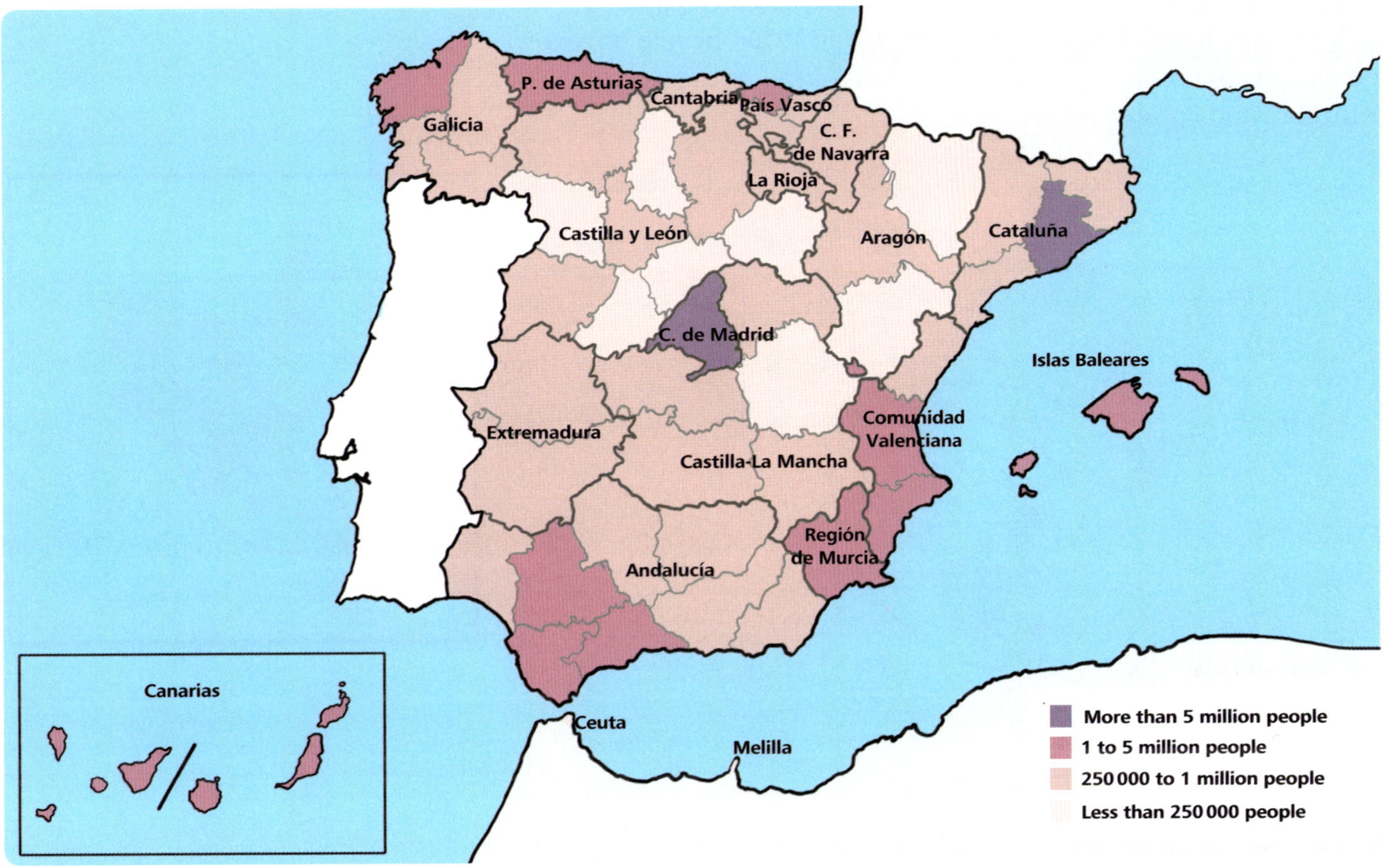

1. Explain why most people live in urban areas.

2. Explain why there are more elderly people now than in the past.

3. How has life expectancy in Spain changed since 1900? What do you think affected this change?

4. Spain's ageing population could have negative consequences in the future. Explain why.

5. Look at the map above and answer the questions.
   a. Does your province have a high or low population?
   b. Which provinces have more than one million inhabitants?
   c. Which province has a higher population: Sevilla or Cantabria?
   d. Which provinces have fewer inhabitants than Barcelona but more than Granada?
   e. Which provinces have more inhabitants than Alicante?

Migrations in Spain

Why do people leave rural areas?

There are three types of migratory movements: **international emigration**, **internal migration** and **international immigration**. During the 20th century, Spain experienced all three.

International emigration

In the first half of the 20th century, many Spaniards **emigrated** to North and South America. In the 1960s and 1970s, people started emigrating to European countries, such as Germany, the United Kingdom and France.

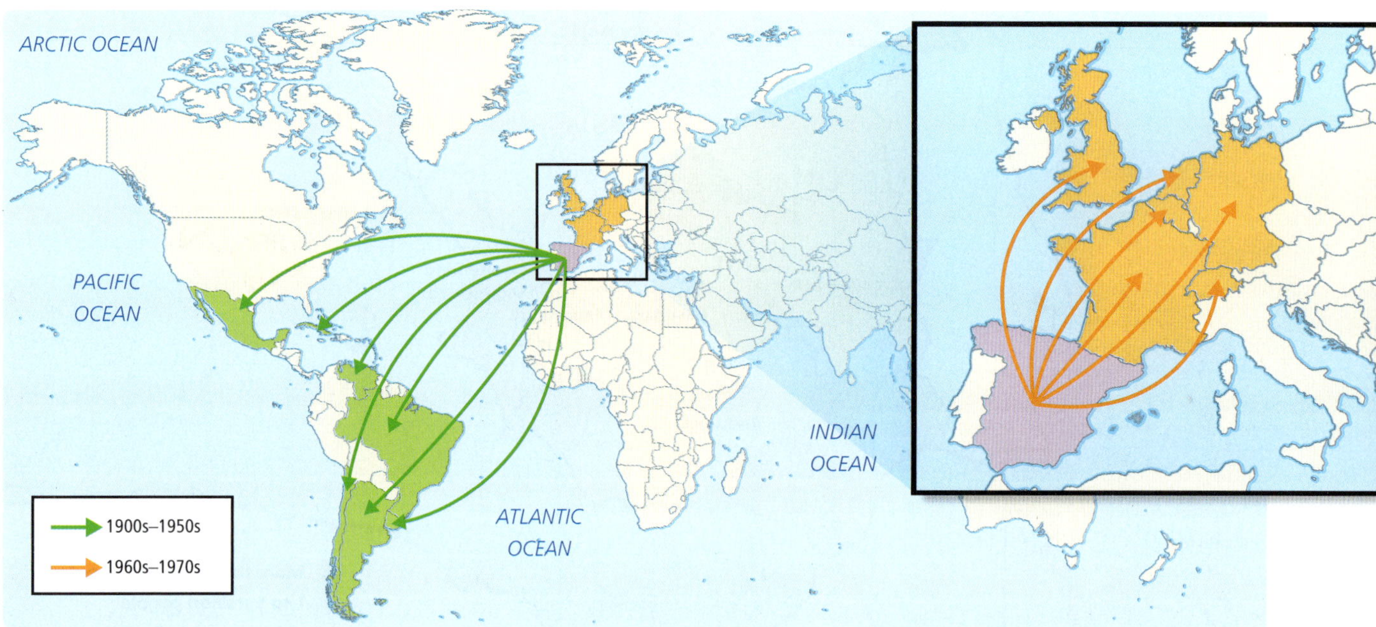

Internal migration

In the second half of the 20th century, about four million people from rural areas moved to cities to find work in factories. This process is known as the **rural exodus**.

The rural exodus can have various consequences:

- overcrowded cities;
- environmental problems, such as air or water pollution;
- high unemployment among rural immigrants;
- lack of food supplies.

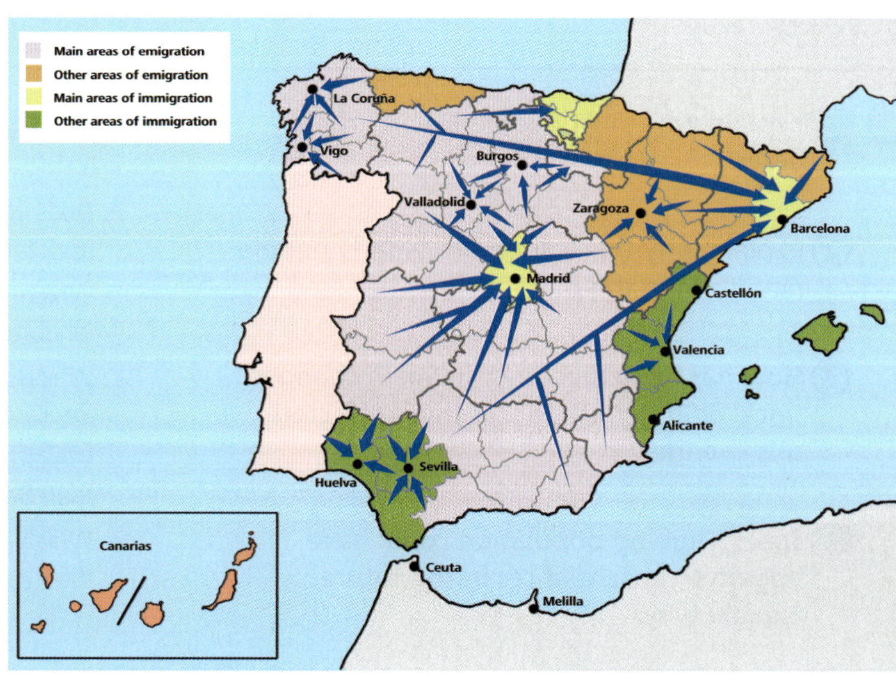

International immigration

At the end of the 20th century the situation changed and Spain started receiving immigrants from other countries. In 2013, there were about 5.6 million immigrants in Spain. Most of them were from Romania, Morocco, Ecuador, Colombia and the United Kingdom.

1 **Analyse the maps on both pages. Read the questions and decide which map will help you to answer them. Then answer them in your notebook.**

a. Which Autonomous Community has the highest number of immigrants?

b. Which Autonomous Communities have fewer immigrants than Cataluña?

c. Which countries did Spaniards migrate to in the first half of the 20th century?

d. What were the main destinations of internal migrations?

e. Which Autonomous Community has a higher number of immigrants: Comunidad Valenciana or Galicia?

f. Which Autonomous Community has more immigrants than Andalucía?

g. Which countries did Spanish people migrate to in the second half of the 20th century?

2 **Find out more about migratory movements nowadays. Are there many people migrating to Spain? Are there many people migrating from Spain? Explain why.**

SCIENCE PROJECT: Population pyramids

We use a graph called a population pyramid to understand how population is distributed in a country or continent. The graph compares the male and female population in different age groups.

- a computer
- Internet access
- a printer
- paper
- a pencil
- a ruler

Aims

- Compare and analyse the different population pyramids.
- Use the census data to draw up a population pyramid for Spain.

Hypothesis

Population growth varies from country to country. Spain's population will have ...

- a population pyramid with a narrow base, or
- a population pyramid with a broad base.

Method

1. Study the population pyramid for Europe (**a**). Identify the three age groups: child, adult and elderly. Which age group is the smallest? And the largest?
2. Label the population pyramids (**b** and **c**) and compare them with the population pyramid for Europe. If necessary, look for the information on the Internet.
   - South America
   - Western Africa
3. What information do these pyramids show about the population in these places? Which age group is the biggest in each of these places? Which age group is the smallest? How do you think the age groups will change in the future?
4. Find information about the male and female population in Spain for 2010. Note down the results in a table. Use them to draw your graph.

a

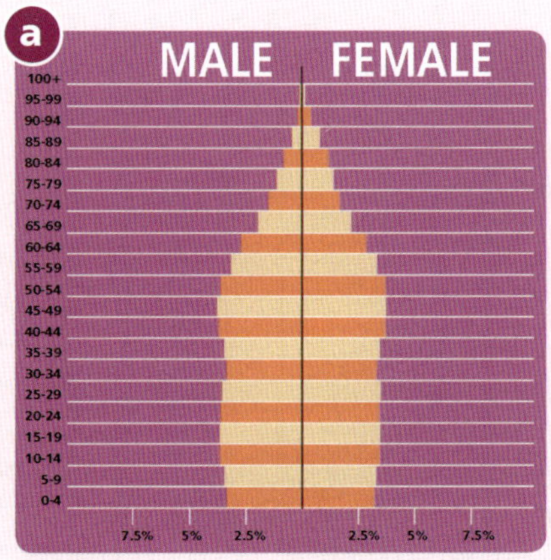

b

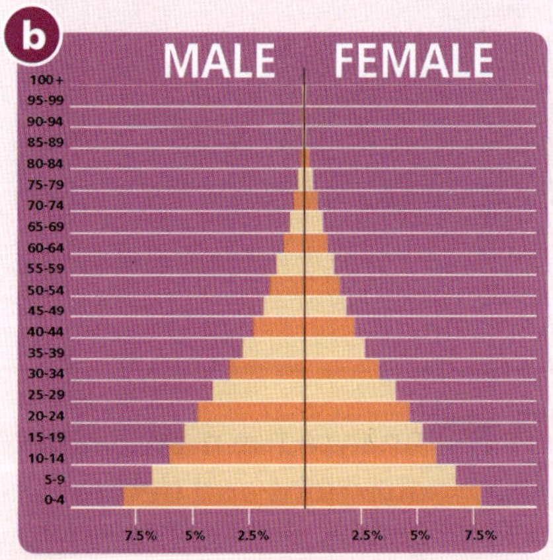

c

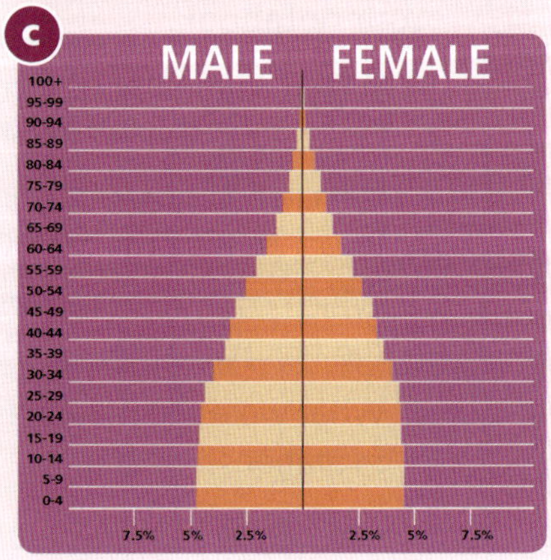

Conclusions

1. Interpret your graph. Describe the Spanish population pyramid.
   a. Is the Spanish population growing? How do you know?
   b. What shape did Spain's population pyramid have in 2010?
   c. Which age group was the biggest? Which age group was the smallest?
2. Why are these graphs called pyramids? Are they always pyramids?

Towards a multicultural society

Societies all over the world have become more multicultural in recent years because of migratory movements.

Throughout history, human beings have migrated in search of greater opportunities and a better life. Europe has a long history of migration. Many Spaniards left the country in the early 20th century and in the 1960s and 1970s, and became immigrants in other countries.

Europe has transformed into a destination for many immigrants in the past few decades. Thousands of people come to Europe (including Spain) from other continents looking for opportunities.

Effects of migratory movements

Immigration can have many positive effects on a country's population. Here are two:

1. **An increase in the economically active population**: many immigrants are of working age.
2. **A higher birth rate**: immigrants are usually adults and, as such, are able to have children.

Migratory movements can have negative effects too. For this reason countries sometimes restrict the number of immigrants that are allowed in. Some people get into a country illegally or by risking their lives. Unfortunately, this can lead to an underground economy.

1. List some of the positive and negative effects of immigration as mentioned above. Can you think of any others?
2. Do you agree with the effects of migratory movements mentioned above?
3. Work with your friend.
   a. Imagine you are an immigrant in Spain. Describe the problems you may have.
   b. You are Spanish and find work in another European country. Describe how you feel. Is living away from home easy or difficult? Why?

Revise

Study skills

1. In your notebook, use the diagram to organise the information about the migrations of Spanish people in the mid-20th century. Then search for information and create a similar diagram about immigrants who came to Spain at the end of the 20th century.

- agricultural crisis
- emigrated
- ships
- lorries
- Belgium
- United Kingdom
- Spaniards
- 1960s and 1970s
- France
- difficult economic situation in Spain
- trains
- Germany
- cars

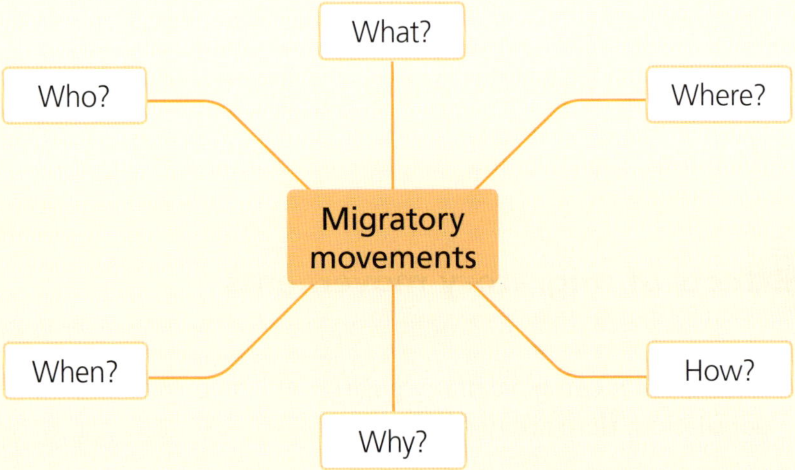

2. Read the text below (A). Then read the text about La Ribera (B) on page 152. In your notebook, write down if the sentences below refer to text A, B or both.

Liverpool is a big city in the north-west of England. Some areas in the city were full of flats and houses because there was a lot of work in the past. But Liverpool lost almost one third of its population in the 1960s and the 1990s. Today, large areas full of houses in different parts of the city are awaiting demolition because of their poor condition. Nobody lives there anymore; the houses and flats are empty. But where some see problems, other people see opportunities. Some neighbourhoods are being renewed and they are transforming empty buildings into shopping or leisure areas. Today, some people in Liverpool are trying to think of possible uses for these areas or buildings, so what was a problem will become part of the solution.

a. This place went into gradual decline in the mid-20th century.

b. Nowadays, this place is abandoned.

c. Some districts in this place have been renewed.

d. Many people moved out to look for job opportunities.

e. This place used to have a large number of inhabitants.

Review

1 Decide if the sentences below are true or false. Correct the false ones in your notebook.

a. We need to know the size of an area and its number of inhabitants to calculate the population density.
b. People only emigrate for economic reasons.
c. If people die, the absolute population decreases.
d. The absolute population increases if there are more births than deaths.
e. Spain's population density is very high.

2 Explain the processes that changed the Spanish population in the 20th century.

a. international emigration
b. internal migration
c. international immigration

3 Look at the diagram and answer the questions in your notebook.

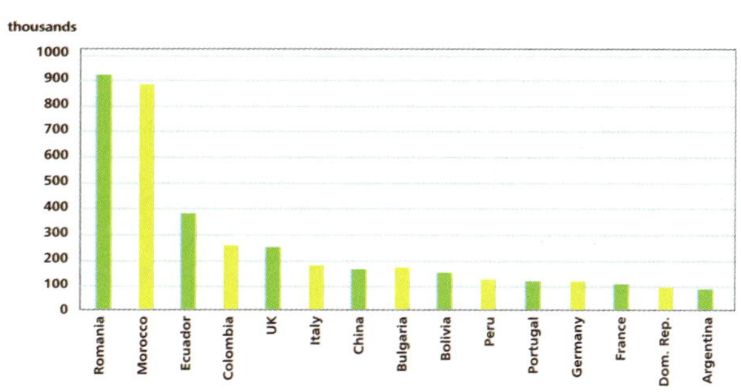

a. Do more people immigrate to Spain from Bolivia or Bulgaria?
b. From which countries do more than 200 000 immigrants come?
c. From which three European countries do most immigrants come?
d. From which three South American countries do most immigrants come?
e. Which four countries do most immigrants who come to Spain emigrate from?

4 Calculate the population density in the different provinces. Use the information in the table.

province	approximate population	approximate surface area (km²)
Murcia	1 470 000	11 300
Ceuta	82 400	18.5
Badajoz	693 900	21 700

5 Talk about the Spanish population. Complete the sentences by giving reasons.

- Population has increased since 1900 .....
- Life expectancy is higher than in 1900 .....
- People leave rural areas .....
- Population density is higher in some areas .....
- Spain has more elderly people .....
- There are many immigrants in Spain .....

6 Complete the summary on page 153.

Checklist

- I can calculate the population density of a place.
- I can explain the migratory movements in Spain.
- I can describe the main characteristics of the Spanish population.
- I can interpret population pyramids.

6 Europe

① Read and discover.

More than 11% of the world's population live in Europe; however, it covers only 7% of the Earth's land area.

Europe has experienced a number of conflicts and wars throughout the centuries. This has led to the creation of a Union within Europe which is today known as the European Union, the aim of which is to promote peace and protect the rights of all citizens. How many countries belong to the EU today?

2. Which continents are bigger than Europe?
3. Look at the largest image and identify the landmarks.
4. Why was the European Union created?
5. Do all European countries belong to the European Union?
6. Have you visited another European country? Which one? What do you know about it?
7. Choose a European country and find out more about it. Answer the questions.
   - What is the capital city?
   - What are the main cities?
   - What languages are spoken?
   - What landforms are there?
   - What typical dishes are there?
   - What traditions are there?
   - What type of political system does it have?

Analyse and organise

1 In your notebook, complete the diagram. Then find out more and add two examples to each category.

- Seine
- Sicily
- Corsica
- Carpathians
- Ireland
- Oder
- Crete
- Apennines
- Pyrenees
- Thames
- Loire
- Alps

Europe

mountains	islands	rivers
......	......	......
......	......	......
......	......	......
......	......	......

2 In your notebook, match the numbers with the landforms from Activity 1. Name the seas.

3 Read the texts and match the headings to the paragraphs. There are two extra headings.

Countries | Climate | Mountains | Territory | Landforms | Capitals

1

Europe's territory covers more than 10 million square kilometres. It reaches the Arctic Circle in the north and the Mediterranean Sea in the south. In the west, it reaches the Atlantic Ocean, and in the east it reaches the Ural Mountains and the Caspian Sea.

2

There have been many disputes over territory in Europe and the borders between countries have often changed. Nowadays, there are 50 different countries. The biggest country is Russia, which covers about 40% of Europe, and the smallest is the Vatican City.

3

Europe can be divided into three different zones. In the centre and north, there are old mountains which are less than 1 000 metres high. In the centre there's a great plain which stretches from the Pyrenees to the Ural Mountains, and in the south there are young mountain chains which are more than 3 000 metres high.

4

Most of the continent is in the temperate climate zone. There's an oceanic climate along the west coast of Europe and a continental climate in the centre and east. In the south, there is a Mediterranean climate and in the far north a polar climate. Finally, there's an alpine climate in the peaks of the mountain chains.

4 Listen to the recording about the Alps and, in your notebook, complete the table.

extension	......
countries	......
highest peak	......
rivers	......
population	......
tourists	......

The population of Europe

Which is the country with the highest population in Europe?

Europe is a very prosperous, highly-populated continent. As a continent, it has the third largest population in the world, after Asia and Africa. About **739 million** people live in Europe, according to a 2013 census.

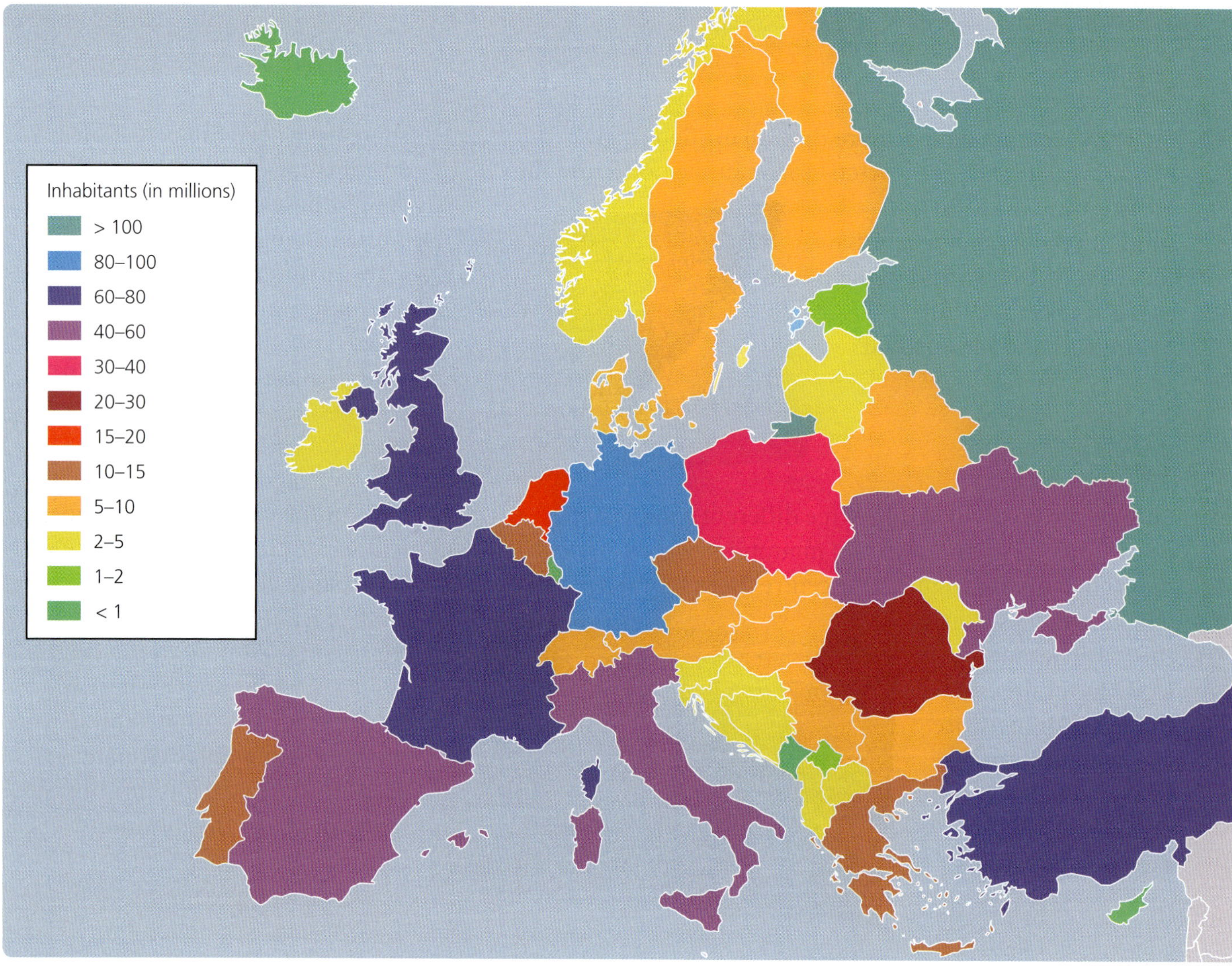

Population distribution

- Europe's population density is about **105 inhabitants per square kilometre**. The countries with the highest population density are Belgium, Italy, Germany, the United Kingdom and the Netherlands. Among the less populated countries in Europe are Norway, Sweden and Finland.
- About 75% of the European population lives in **urban areas**. The biggest cities are Moscow, Paris, London, Madrid, Berlin, Rome and Athens.

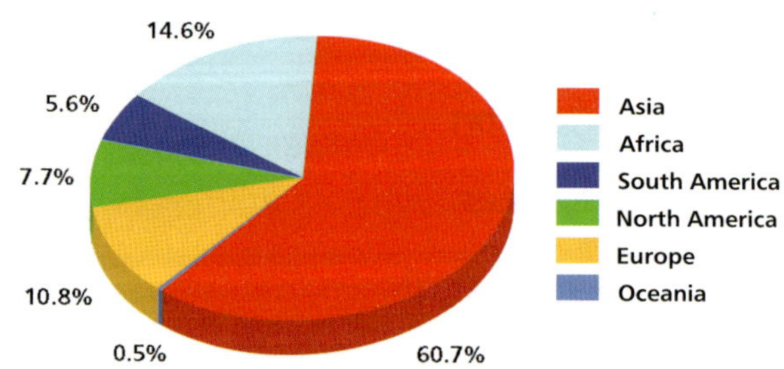

World population by continent

Ageing population

- In Europe, the **birth rate** is low but the **death rate** is also low. Average life expectancy in Europe is now around **80 years**.
- There has been a slowing down in the **natural increase**, because women in Europe have fewer children than in previous decades.
- Europe is an **ageing continent**: the number of people over 65 is almost the same as the number of young people. In the future, there will be more people who need pensions and healthcare and there will be fewer people to pay for them.
- Despite being an ageing continent, Europe's population is still growing, mainly due to **migratory movements**. The arrival of immigrants is causing the population of Europe to grow.

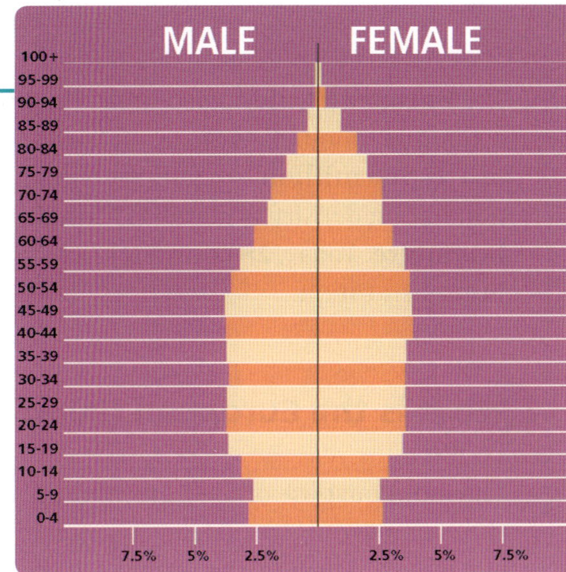

Population pyramid of Europe

Cultural diversity

- Europe is also a **multicultural** continent. There is a great diversity of cultures, beliefs and traditions. More than 200 languages are spoken in Europe. The main languages are Russian, German, French, English, Italian and Spanish.

1. Compare the Spanish population with Europe as a whole. Consider the following:
   - population density
   - natural growth and ageing
   - migration
   - life expectancy
2. Use the map on page 88 to identify the countries with the highest and lowest populations.
3. Why is the European population getting older?

Link it up

Compare the European population pyramid with the Spanish population pyramid that you made in Unit 5. Are they similar?

The European Union

How many countries belong to the EU?

The **European Union**, also called the **EU**, is a political and economic union of countries in Europe. It has a population of over **500 million** inhabitants with a very high population density of about **117 inhabitants per square kilometre**. Today, **28 countries** belong to the European Union.

What is the European Union?

The main purpose of the European Union is to improve the economic and social development of the member states and to protect the rights of EU citizens. The EU has a system of common laws, which ensure free movement of people, goods, services and capital.

The EU was created in **1957** to promote economic cooperation (**Treaty of Rome**). At first, it was called the **European Economic Community** (**EEC**). Since then, it has become a single economic market with the **euro** as its official currency.

The first member states were France, Italy, Germany, the Netherlands, Belgium and Luxembourg.

In **1993**, the EEC became the European Union (**Maastricht Treaty**). The member countries wanted to strengthen economic ties while also forming a new, political union.

Today, **political policies** are very important in the EU. Economic and political decisions affect all the countries and shared systems of justice and security are being developed too.

With **24 official languages**, there is great social and cultural diversity in the EU.

EU citizens can move freely within the European Union. They can live, study or work in any other country in the EU.

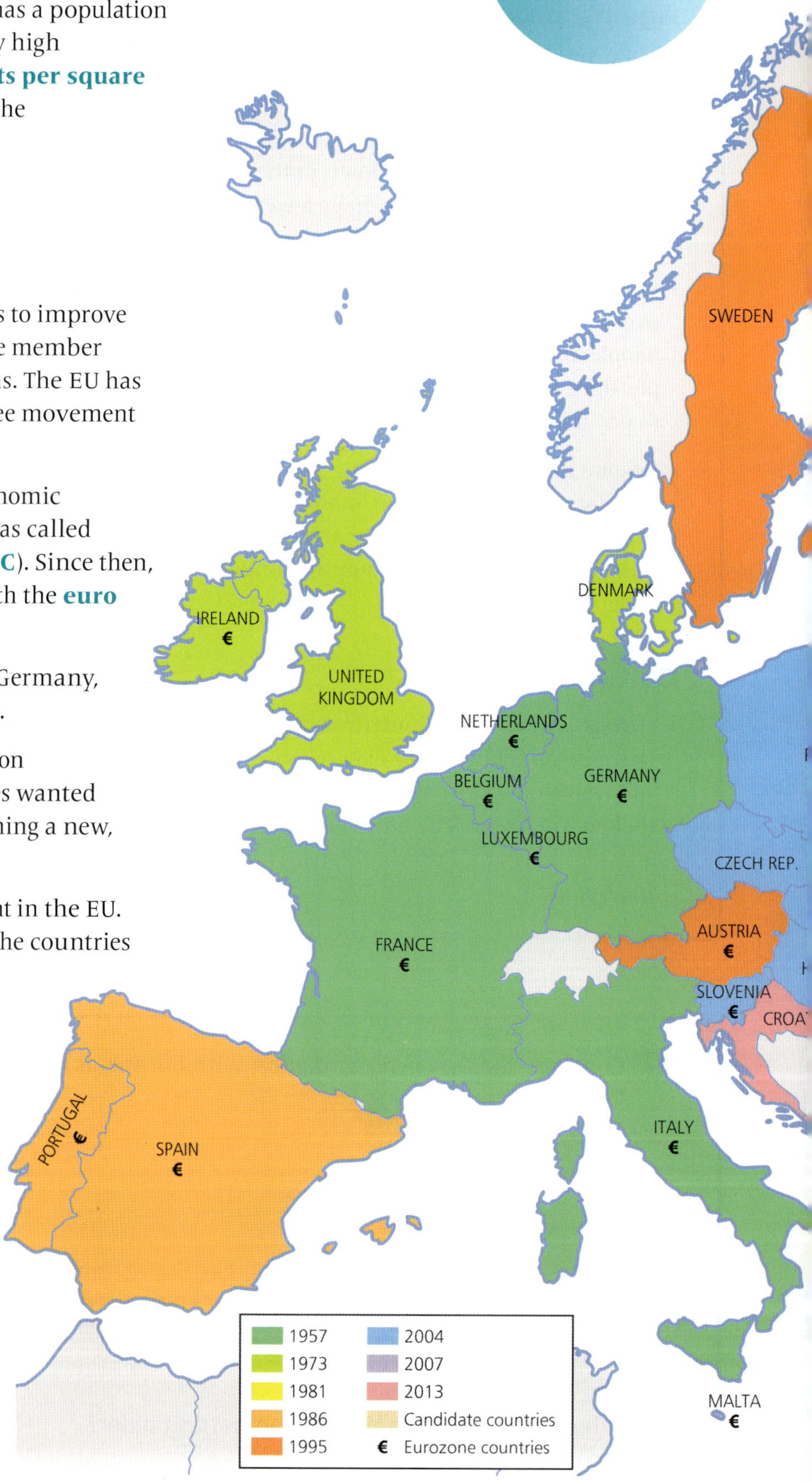

Did you know?

The EU's motto is 'United in diversity'. What do you think this motto means?

EU symbols

The euro

- The euro is the currency of the **Eurozone**. It is the official currency in 18 countries, including Spain.
- Spain adopted the euro in **2002**.

The EU flag

- The 12 stars on the **EU flag** arranged in a circle represent unity between the member countries.
- You can see the EU flag in front of public buildings, on coins, banknotes and car number plates.

Ode to Joy

- *Ode to Joy* is the European anthem. It is based on a melody from the 9th Symphony by Ludwig van Beethoven.

1. What is the main purpose of the European Union?
2. Note down the countries of the Eurozone. What are the advantages of a single currency?
3. When did Spain join the European Union? When did it adopt the euro?
4. In 1993, the Single European Market came into force. What do you think the benefits of a single economic market are?
5. Compare the population density of Spain and the European Union. Which has a higher population density?

How the EU is organised

Find Strasbourg, Brussels and Luxembourg City on the map.

European Union institutions

These are the six main **institutions** in the EU. They are based in different EU cities.

1

European Parliament

- **Place**: Strasbourg (France).
- **Institution**: It is the legislative body directly elected by EU citizens.
- **Function**: It prepares and passes laws and budgets. It shares legislative and budgetary powers with the Council of the European Union.

2

Council of the EU

- **Place**: Brussels (Belgium).
- **Institution**: It is the legislative body formed by the 28 ministers (one per member state).
- **Function**: It coordinates economic and defence policies and signs agreements between the EU and other countries.

3

European Council

- **Place**: Brussels (Belgium).
- **Institution**: It is the strategic body of the EU. It is formed by the heads of state or government of the member states.
- **Function**: It sets the EU's general political direction.

Link it up

Compare the division of powers in the EU and in Spain. What are the similarities?

Look at Unit 4.

4 European Commission

- **Place**: Brussels (Belgium).
- **Institution**: It is the executive body of the EU, formed by 28 members (one per member state).
- **Function**: It implements EU policies, spends EU funds and presents proposals for new European laws.

5 Court of Justice of the EU

- **Place**: Luxembourg City (Luxembourg).
- **Institution**: It is the highest court in the EU legal system.
- **Function**: It ensures that the law is observed in all member states.

6 European Court of Auditors

- **Place**: Luxembourg City (Luxembourg).
- **Institution**: It is an audit agency.
- **Function**: It ensures that EU funds are invested properly.

1. Which country is the newest member of the European Union? When did it join the EU? Find it on the map.
2. Which institutions pass laws and budgets?
3. Explain the main differences between the Council of the EU and the European Commission.
4. In your notebook, answer the questions.
   a. Which institutions are based in Brussels?
   b. Which institution has judicial power?
   c. Which institution has members who are elected by European citizens?
5. Find out about the European Central Bank. What functions does it perform? Where is it based?

SCIENCE PROJECT: Countries of the EU

Aims

- Find information about three countries in the EU.
- Compare the results and make a presentation.

- a computer
- Internet access
- a printer
- paper
- a pencil
- a ruler

Method

1. Look at the table. What is similar or different in these countries? Locate the countries on a map.

	Ireland	Sweden	Poland
location	Northern Europe	Northern Europe	Central Europe
capital city	Dublin	Stockholm	Warsaw
languages	English, Irish	Swedish	Polish
climate	oceanic	continental, polar	continental
geography	mountains and hills on the coast, lowland in the interior	mountains in the west, lakes in the south	flat, part of the North European Plain, mountains in the south
industry	pharmaceutical and chemical products, computers	wood and paper products, electronic equipment, cars	heavy machinery, iron and coal

2. Choose three EU countries. Investigate and find information about them. Make your own table and complete it with the results. Compare the three countries.
3. Make a presentation. Illustrate it with photos and maps.

Warsaw

Stockholm

Dublin

Conclusions

1. What similarities and differences did you identify in the three countries that you have chosen?
2. What did you find out about these countries that you didn't know? What surprised you?
3. How do these countries compare to Spain?

EU citizens' rights

The European Union is based on the values of democracy, freedom, equality and respect for human rights. Any person with the nationality of a member state of the European Union is automatically a citizen of the EU. European citizenship does not replace your nationality. It does however give you a set of additional rights. These include the right to:

- Move freely within the EU.
- Live and work in any country in the EU.
- Vote in elections to the European Parliament.
- Be protected by the diplomatic authorities of any EU country.

The European Ombudsman

The European Union has created the post of **Ombudsman**, whose responsibility is to represent the interests of EU citizens. The Ombudsman investigates and responds to complaints from EU citizens against EU institutions, offices and agencies. The Ombudsman's office is independent and doesn't depend on any government. Any EU citizen can send a complaint to the European Ombudsman if they suffer discrimination, are treated unfairly or are refused information.

1. Why is the Ombudsman important? Does it exist in Spain?
2. Find out more about the rights of EU citizens. In your notebook, classify them into four groups.
   - civil rights
   - political rights
   - economic rights
   - social and cultural rights
3. EU citizenship is also about responsibilities. What duties do you think EU citizens have?
4. Discuss the following issues with a partner.
   - Compare the rights of EU citizens with the rights of Spanish citizens.
   - Can people develop a good public-spirited attitude?
   - Can you teach others to be more public-spirited and socially responsible? How?

Study skills

1 In your notebook, make a timeline about the European Union. Include the dates in the box.

- 1957
- 1993
- 1981
- 1986
- 1995
- 2004
- 2007
- 2002
- 2013
- 1973

The European Economic Community was created.	.....	.....	.....	.....

1957	.....	.....	.....	.....	.....	.....	.....	.....	.....

.....	.....	.....	.....	.....

2 Read the text below (A). Then read the text about Europe Day (B) on page 152. In your notebook, decide whether the sentences below refer to text A, B or both.

Each year the European Union chooses the European Capitals of Culture. The main objective of this programme is to show the richness and diversity of Europe. For the whole year, these cities organise a number of cultural events that bring people from different countries together to learn about each other's culture, values and beliefs. The European Capital of Culture initiative was created in 1985. Since then more than 40 cities have been elected, including Madrid, Amsterdam, Stockholm, Prague and Lisbon.

a. This initiative consists of organising different cultural events.

b. It is celebrated on 9 May.

c. It commemorates the beginning of the European Union.

d. Its origins go back to the 1980s.

Review

1 Look at the map and, follow the instructions.

a. Find the place where the European Commission is based.
b. Point to the first member states of the EU.
c. Point to the countries that joined the EU in 2007.
d. Find the capital cities of the EU member states.

2 Compare the population pyramid of Europe for 1950 with the pyramid on page 89.

a. What changes do you see in the younger population from 1950 to 2010?
b. What changes do you see in the older population from 1950 to 2010?
c. What consequences do you think these changes will have for our society?

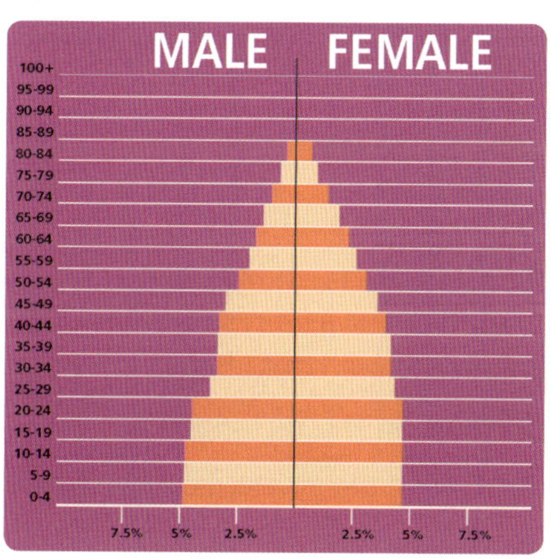

3 In your notebook, identify whether the following numbers refer to the population of Europe, the European Union or Spain.

a. 93 inhabitants per km^2
b. 117 inhabitants per km^2
c. 105 inhabitants per km^2
d. 46 million
e. 500 million
f. 739 million

4 Read the questions and decide if you are for or against each idea. Justify your answers.

a. Should all the countries in the EU use the same currency?
b. Should the member states reintroduce passport controls on their borders?
c. Should all European countries belong to the EU?

5 Talk about the European Union. Use the diagram to help you.

The EU
- six institutions
- 24 official languages
- 28 member states
- in 1957
- over 500 million inhabitants

6 Complete the summary on page 153.

Checklist

- I can describe the main characteristics of populations in Europe and the EU.
- I can identify the European Union's main objectives.
- I can identify European institutions and name the functions they perform.

TEAMWORK Population problems

1 Are these statements true or false? Correct the false ones in your notebook.

a. A positive natural increase means the birth rate is higher than the death rate.

b. A negative natural increase means the death rate is lower than the birth rate.

c. Population density shows us how populated an area is.

d. Overpopulation occurs when a population's density exceeds the capacity of the environment to supply the needs of individuals.

e. Overpopulation is caused by an excessive increase in the birth rate.

2 Look at the photos. How can overpopulation affect people's quality of life?

3 Read and discuss. Justify your answers.

1 Life expectancy is ..... live.

a. the number of years you

b. the average number of years people

c. the number of years your family

2 Life expectancy in Spain is .....

a. higher than in African countries.

b. lower than in African countries.

c. the same as in African countries.

3 An ageing population implies an increase in the percentage of .....

a. elderly people.

b. adults.

c. children.

4 What could occur as a result of an ageing population? There could be .....

a. a decrease in the birth rate.

b. a decrease in the economically active population.

c. a decrease in life expectancy.

Group project

The whole is greater than the sum of its parts.

④ Look at the photos. Which of the things shown have contributed to an increase in life expectancy? How?

a
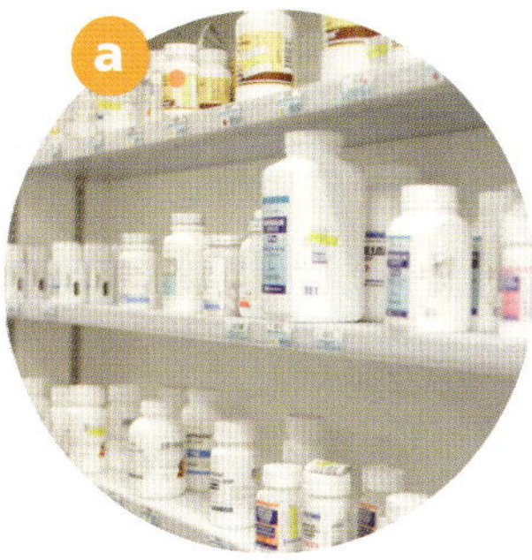
b

c
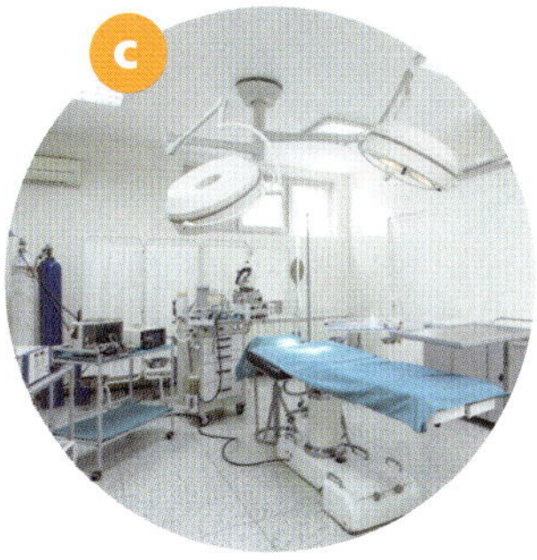
d

⑤ In groups, make a slide presentation about an overpopulated country. Your presentation should include the following information:

- Your chosen country, for example:
  - China
  - India
  - Indonesia
  - Nigeria
- Relevant data from your chosen country, such as:
  - births
  - deaths
  - immigrants
  - emigrants
- Statistics on:
  - natural increase
  - actual increase
  - population density
- The distribution of population in the country.
- The problems overpopulation causes in the country.

Use the Internet to look for pictures and relevant information. Keep the information on each slide to a minimum. Remember to include a reference list.

Checklist

- All group members contributed actively to the project.
- We calculated the natural increase, the actual increase and the population density.
- We considered the main problems that overpopulation causes in the chosen country.
- We searched for new information from various sources.

Quick quiz

1 Listen to the quiz and choose the correct answer from the options.

1	a. deputies	b. senators	c. Prime Minister
2	a. 19	b. 17	c. 18
3	a. America	b. Germany	c. France
4	a. rural	b. coastal	c. mountainous
5	a. 75%	b. 97%	c. 58%
6	a. 30	b. 24	c. 15

2 Listen and check your answers.

A

B

C

D

Extended quiz

3 Read the quiz and write your ideas in your notebook.

1. What type of political system is there in Spain?
2. What three areas of power does the Spanish Constitution establish?
3. What population groups can you see in photos A–D?
4. How many inhabitants did Spain have in 1900?
5. What is the average life expectancy in Europe?
6. When was the EU created?

4 Listen to this student's answers. Match them to questions 1 to 6 in Activity 3.

5 Now listen to the answers in order. Check your original ideas from Activity 3.

Team test!

① Get into teams. Take turns to guess the words for definitions 1–9.

Team A

1. ····· : the most important law in Spain.
2. ····· : a member of the Congress.
3. ····· : one of the symbols of Spain. It is called *La Marcha Real*.
4. ····· : a person who goes to a different country to live there.
5. ····· : the average number of years that a person lives.
6. ····· : the number of inhabitants in Spain.
7. ····· : the European anthem.
8. ····· : the number of stars on the European flag.
9. ····· : one of the institutions of the EU. It is the executive body of the EU.
10. ····· : ______________________.

Team B

1. ····· : one of the houses in the Spanish Parliament. It consists of senators.
2. ····· : the highest court in Spain.
3. ····· : the Spanish national motto.
4. ····· : the difference between the number of births and the number of deaths.
5. ····· : Spain's population density.
6. ····· : movement of people from rural areas to urban areas.
7. ····· : the number of countries that use the euro.
8. ····· : the country that joined the European Union in 2013.
9. ····· : one of the EU institutions. It is based in Strasbourg.
10. ····· : ______________________.

② Listen and check your answers.

③ Now, in your notebook, invent a tenth definition. Ask someone from the other team to guess the words for definitions 1–10.

7 The Middle Ages

① Read and discover.

During the Middle Ages, different civilisations lived on the Iberian Peninsula. Visigoths settled after the Roman Empire fell. Then Muslims invaded, calling their new territories Al-Andalus. Here, three religious groups lived together: Muslims, Jews and Christians. Over the next centuries, the Christians in the north fought against the Muslims. By the end of 1492, the whole Iberian Peninsula was under Christian rule again. What was the period before the Middle Ages called?

2. What were the three main civilisations on the Iberian Peninsula during the Middle Ages?

3. Look at the images on both pages. Identify the three civilisations and put them in chronological order.

4. When did the Middle Ages in Spain start and end?

5. What three religions were present in medieval Spain?

6. Which religions are the words below related to? Explain what they mean. If necessary, search for the information on the Internet.
   - church
   - the Koran
   - synagogue
   - the Torah
   - mosque
   - cathedral
   - the Bible

7. In terms of religious tolerance, is Spanish society today similar to that of Al-Andalus?

Analyse and organise

1 Read about the periods in Spanish history that you have learnt about so far. Then organise the information using the model diagram.

	Prehistory 2 000 000 years ago – 6 000 years ago (invention of writing)		Ancient history 6 000 years ago (invention of writing) – the fall of the Roman Empire (AD 476)	
periods	Palaeolithic period	Neolithic period	pre-Roman tribes	Roman Hispania
characteristics	nomads, clans, simple stone tools, clothes made of animal skins, cave paintings	first settlements, agriculture, woollen clothes, megaliths, tools made of stone and bone	tribes (the Celts and the Iberians), stone-wall settlements, tools made of metal, trade	Romanisation, Latin, calendars, Christianity, aqueducts, stone roads, sewage systems

2 Classify the photos according to the period they belong to.

a

b

c

d

e

f

3 Read the text and decide if the sentences below are true or false.

Visigothic Kingdom

San Pedro de la Nave, Zamora

The Middle Ages began in the 5th century when four Germanic tribes, the Visigoths, the Suebi, the Vandals and the Alans settled in Hispania.

In the 6th century, the Visigoths conquered the other three tribes, which gave them control of most of the Iberian Peninsula. To unite the country, the Visigoths established the capital of their kingdom in **Toledo** and adopted some of the Roman ways of life. They learnt Latin and followed Roman laws. They did, however, keep some of their own customs too. In AD 589 the Visigoth king, Recaredo I, converted his kingdom to Catholicism during the Third Council of Toledo.

Visigothic society consisted of a king, nobles and peasants. The nobles came from wealthy families, often relatives of the king, who owned land and had considerable power. The king and nobles held councils to discuss any problems in the kingdom. The rest of the population were mostly peasants, who worked in the countryside on nobles' land in exchange for food and a place to live. The Visigoths built small stone churches and were excellent metal workers.

a. Four Germanic tribes settled in Hispania after the fall of the Roman Empire.

b. Rome was the capital city of the Visigothic Kingdom.

c. The Visigoths converted to Catholicism in the 6th century.

d. The Visigoths adopted some Roman customs, but they also kept their own customs.

e. Peasants didn't make money.

4 Listen to the recording about the Visigoths. Complete the sentences in your notebook.

- The Visigoths were a *Slavic/Germanic* tribe.
- They *built/didn't build* cities.
- Some examples of Visigothic architecture can be found in the *north/east* of Spain.
- The Treasure of Guarrazar is a collection of more than *twenty/two hundred* crowns and gold crosses.
- The *Muslims/Romans* invaded the Visigothic Kingdom in AD 711.
- San Isidoro de Sevilla wrote a famous *encyclopedia/poem*.

Al-Andalus

What was the most important city in Al-Andalus?

In the 8th century, the Iberian Peninsula was invaded by Muslims. Soon they created one of the most advanced societies in Europe.

The Muslim invasion

In AD **711**, Muslims from North Africa invaded Visigothic Spain. After the **Battle of Guadalete**, in which the Visigoths were defeated, Muslim armies continued the conquest. In just a few years they conquered most of the Iberian Peninsula and the Balearic Islands. The only remaining Christian territory was in the north of the peninsula. The Muslims called their conquered territory **Al-Andalus**. At first, Al-Andalus was a province that depended on the Caliph of Damascus. Then, in 756, Abd al-Rahman I established the **Emirate of Córdoba** and proclaimed himself **emir**. In AD 929, Al-Andalus became independent. Abd al-Rahman III established the **Caliphate of Córdoba**. He was the first **caliph** and the greatest ruler of Al-Andalus.

Economy and society

Al-Andalus society consisted of three religious groups: **Muslims**, **Christians** and **Jews**. Most people in Al-Andalus lived in walled towns and cities. Their main activities were crafts and trade. The **medina**, where the craftspeople lived, and the market place, called the **zoco**, were in the centre of the city. People prayed in a mosque, or **mezquita**. Also inside the city walls, there was usually a fort called an **alcazaba** and a fortified palace called an **alcázar**. The cities were surrounded by fields where farmers grew cereals, olives and grapes.

The legacy of Al-Andalus

The Muslims gave a lot to Spain. Perhaps the most important contribution from the people of Al-Andalus was their knowledge. They were responsible for great advances in medicine, astronomy and mathematics. They introduced paper, the compass and Arabic numerals, a numerical system which was at this time revolutionary due to its inclusion of the number zero. They also built libraries and established universities. The Muslims also developed new methods of irrigation and introduced new crops, such as rice, oranges and aubergines.

Link it up

The compass was probably invented in China but it was introduced in Europe thanks to the Muslims. What is a compass used for?

Look at Unit 2.

1. Explain the functions of the following parts of the city in Al-Andalus:
   - alcazaba
   - zoco
   - medina
   - mezquita
   - walls
   - alcázar
2. Many Spanish words are of Arabic origin. Search for some examples.
3. Explain the importance of the advances listed below. Imagine what life was like in the 8th century. How would it have been different to life today?
   - paper
   - library
   - compass
   - university
   - irrigation
   - numerical system

Christian Kingdoms

Do you think the process of reconquering the Peninsula was easy? Why?

The **Reconquista** began just after the Muslim conquest in the 8th century and finished with the conquest of the Kingdom of Granada in 1492.

Stages of the Reconquista

Between the 8th and 10th centuries, the Christians from the north of the Iberian Peninsula created small kingdoms that were independent of Al-Andalus. In AD **722**, don Pelayo, the ruler of the Kingdom of Asturias, defeated the Muslim army at the **Battle of Covadonga**. This victory marked the beginning of the Reconquista.

In the 11th century, Al-Andalus was divided into small independent states called **taifas**. The taifas were in constant conflict, which helped the Christians from the north expand into the south and reconquer Muslim territories. In **1085**, Alfonso VI, the king of León and Castilla, conquered **Toledo**.

Soon, the Christian Kingdoms united and, as a result, became bigger and stronger. In **1212**, the combined forces of the Kingdoms of Aragón, Navarra, Castilla and Portugal defeated the Muslims at the **Battle of Las Navas de Tolosa**. This battle was a key victory in the Reconquista. Soon, the kings of Castilla conquered Andalucía: Fernando III conquered Sevilla and Córdoba, and his son Alfonso X, conquered Jerez, Cádiz and Murcia. At the same time, the king of Aragón, Jaime I conquered Valencia and the Balearic Islands.

In **1469**, king **Fernando II** of Aragón and queen **Isabel I** of Castilla married and united their two kingdoms creating one powerful Christian Kingdom. In **1492**, the Christians finally conquered the Kingdom of Granada.

Repopulation

The Reconquista was a complex process that involved not only fighting, but also the repopulation of areas previously occupied by the Muslims. It went through four stages:

- the Duero Valley;
- areas between the Ebro and the Tajo;
- the Guadiana and Turia Valleys;
- Andalucía and Murcia.

Feudalism was a hierarchical social system that was used in the Middle Ages. Medieval society consisted of the king and four other groups of people.

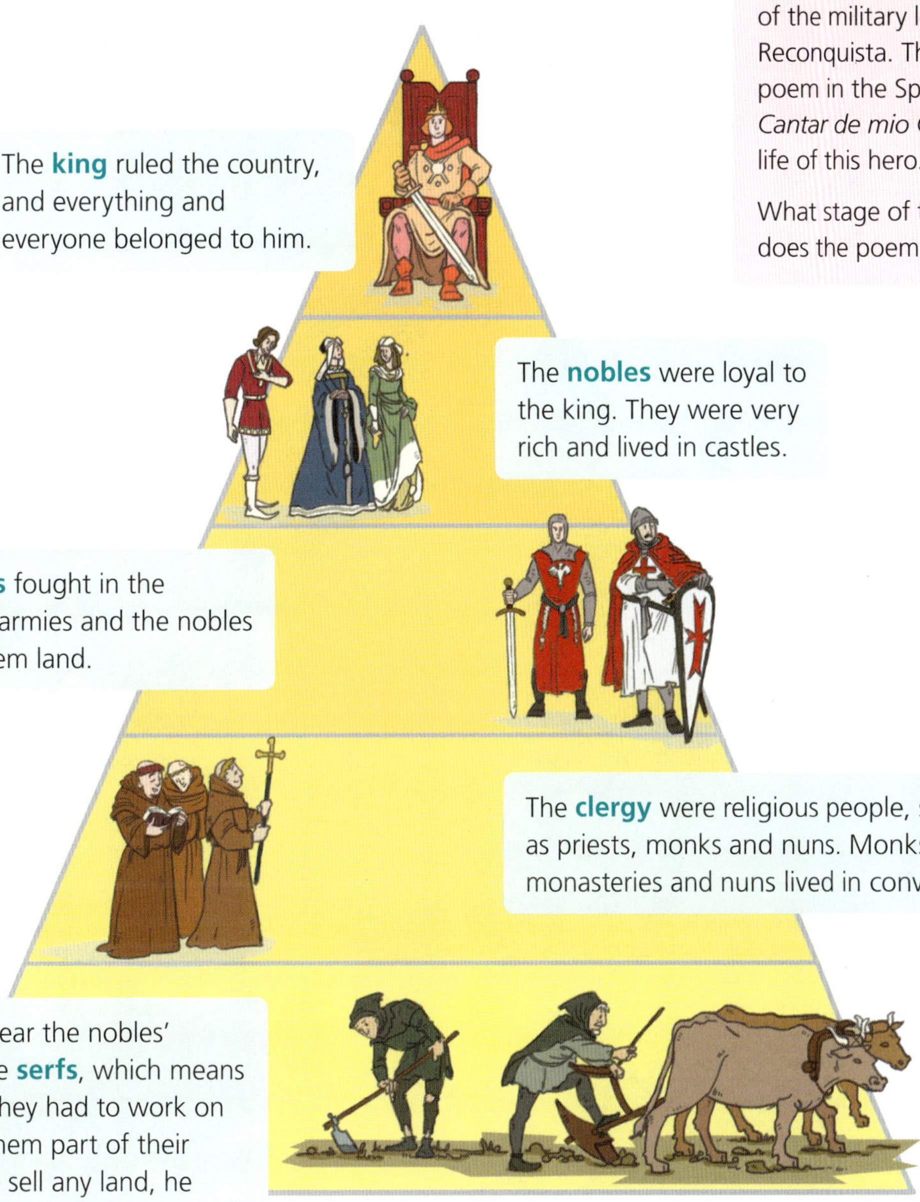

The **king** ruled the country, and everything and everyone belonged to him.

The **nobles** were loyal to the king. They were very rich and lived in castles.

Knights fought in the nobles' armies and the nobles gave them land.

The **clergy** were religious people, such as priests, monks and nuns. Monks lived in monasteries and nuns lived in convents.

Peasants lived in villages near the nobles' castles. Most peasants were **serfs**, which means they weren't free people. They had to work on the nobles' land and give them part of their crops. If a noble decided to sell any land, he sold the serfs along with it.

Did you know?

Rodrigo Díaz, or El Cid, was one of the military leaders of the Reconquista. The oldest epic poem in the Spanish language *Cantar de mio Cid* is based on the life of this hero.

What stage of the Reconquista does the poem describe?

1. Order the events and write the dates in your notebook. Then make a timeline.
   - the conquest of the Kingdom of Granada
   - the Battle of Covadonga
   - the conquest of Toledo
   - the Battle of Guadalete
   - the Battle of Las Navas de Tolosa

2. Classify the words using the pyramid. Some of them can belong to more than one group. Justify your answers.
   - army
   - convent
   - land
   - monastery
   - serfs
   - castle

Medieval cities

Medieval cities usually developed around a castle. Why?

In the 12th century, trade started to expand. As a result, cities grew and became more important. New cities were usually built near trade routes, such as roads and rivers.

Medieval cities were protected by a **large wall**. Townspeople and travellers had to enter and leave the city through **fortified gateways**.

The streets were very narrow and the wooden houses were close together, which meant fire was a great danger. Diseases spread very quickly because people lived in bad conditions, and there was no running water in the houses and no sewage system.

Important buildings, such as the **cathedral** and the **town hall**, were in the main square. The main square was also where the market and fairs took place. **Craftspeople** and **artisans** made products which were bought and sold by **merchants**.

The majority of people who lived in cities were merchants and craftspeople. Craftspeople who did the same type of work joined together to form **guilds**. These guilds became very powerful in the city. They controlled the prices of the products and the quality of work.

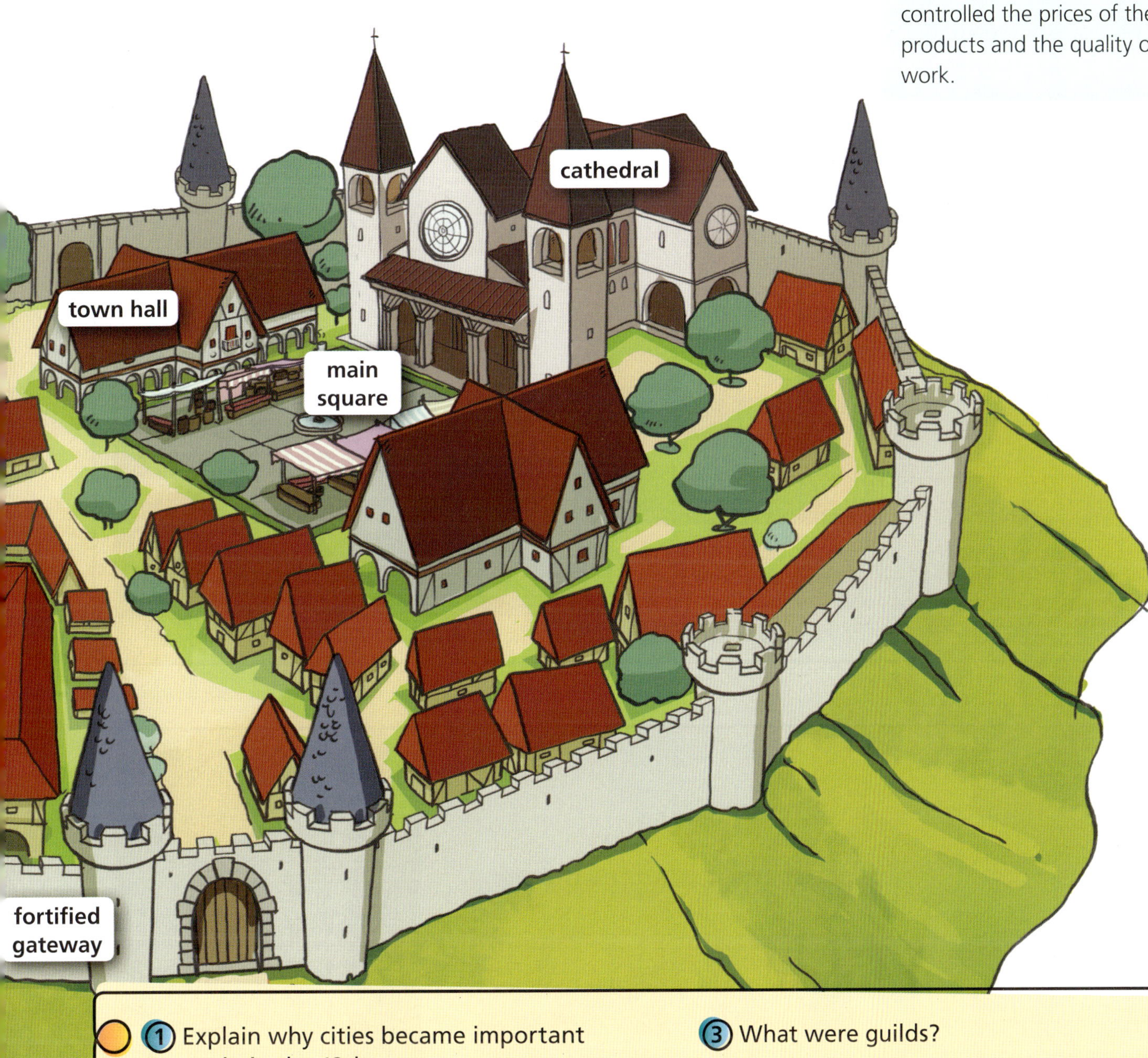

1. Explain why cities became important again in the 12th century.
2. Compare a medieval city with a city in Al-Andalus.
3. What were guilds?
4. Explain why the lack of running water and a sewage system affected people's health.

Art in the Middle Ages

Have you ever seen any examples of the four architectural styles shown in the photos?

Spanish medieval art is varied due to the influence of the different civilisations on the Iberian Peninsula during the period, especially the Christians and Muslims. We can identify four main styles of medieval art in Spain: **Islamic**, **Romanesque**, **Gothic** and **Mudéjar**.

Islamic style

After the Muslim conquest of the Iberian Peninsula, Spanish artists worked in the **Islamic** style.

Characteristics:

- horseshoe arches
- harmonious proportions
- mosaics
- patterns using a repetition of geometric and natural motifs
- domes
- open courtyards
- no sculptures
- bright colours

The Great Mosque of Córdoba

The Aljafería Palace in Zaragoza

The Alhambra in Granada

Romanesque style

Artists in Christian territories during the 11th and 12th centuries used the **Romanesque** style.

Characteristics:

- small windows
- rounded arches
- thick walls
- low structures
- dark inside

The church of San Martín in Palencia

The church of San Clemente of Tahull in Lérida

Gothic style

Churches and cathedrals were built in the **Gothic** style between the 13th and 16th centuries.

Characteristics:

- big stained-glass windows showing scenes from the Bible
- pointed arches
- thin walls
- tall structures
- rose windows

The Cathedral of Burgos

The Cathedral of Toledo

Mudéjar style

In the Christian Kingdoms, Islamic style was mixed with the Romanesque or Gothic styles creating a new type of art called **Mudéjar**. This style developed in the 12th century.

The Cathedral of Teruel

The Alcázar of Sevilla

1. Spanish culture of the Middle Ages was also influenced by the Jewish community. In which Spanish cities can we find Jewish quarters?

2. Look at the photos and identify the style.

a 

b 

c 

d 

SCIENCE PROJECT: The City of Three Cultures

Aim

Plan a trip around the City of Three Cultures (Toledo).

Method

- a printable map of Toledo
- a notebook
- a pen
- a pencil
- a computer
- Internet access

1. Look at the map of Toledo and locate the main monuments.
2. The map shows the different monuments that illustrate the coexistence of Christians, Muslims and Jews.
3. Use the Internet to find more information about each monument.
   - What type of monument is it?
   - When was it built?
   - What style is it (Islamic/Romanesque/Gothic/Mudéjar)?
   - Is it possible to visit it? If so, what are the opening hours?
   - How long does a typical visit take?
   - How much do tickets cost?
4. Search for photos of the monuments.
5. Depending on the information that you have found, plan a visit around Toledo. Take into account the following:
   - You must begin at the starting point (see below).
   - You are visiting the city on a Saturday.
   - You have a budget of 50 euros.
   - You arrive in Toledo at 10 am. The bus leaves you near the Puerta de Bisagra.
   - You should visit at least one monument belonging to each culture (Christian, Muslim, Jewish).
   - You leave Toledo at 4 pm from the car park near the Monasterio de San Juan de los Reyes.
6. On a photocopy of the map, mark the route you are going to follow.

The Puerta de Bisagra

Conclusions

1. What monuments are you going to see?
2. What did you learn about the monuments you have chosen?
3. Prepare a short presentation using the information and the photos you have found.
4. Share your trip plan with your classmates.

The coexistence of three religions

The society in Al-Andalus was very diverse and consisted of people with different religions.

- The **Muslims** were the most powerful group. They owned the best land and were in charge of the government.
- The **Muladi** were Christians who converted to Islam. Some of them followed the Muslim religion to avoid paying taxes.
- The **Mozarabs** were Christians who kept their own religion but adopted Muslim customs.
- The **Jews** were a minority but they played an important role in politics, commerce and art. They lived in separate districts called *juderías*.

The Muslims of Al-Andalus were respectful of other people's beliefs. They allowed Christians and Jews to practise their religions. Muslims, Christians and Jews often lived peacefully in Muslim cities.

The cathedral in Zaragoza

The mosque in Córdoba

The synagogue in Toledo

The Jewish quarter in Córdoba

1. What were the main groups in Al-Andalus society?
2. Do you think the coexistence of these groups was always easy? Why? Think of the possible problems that might have developed.
3. What happened to Muslim mosques after the Reconquista?
4. The Toledo School of Translators was a group of Jewish, Muslim and Christian scholars. They translated the most important scientific and philosophical works of ancient and medieval times. Explain why their work was important.

Revise

Study skills

1. Complete the diagram in your notebook with one of the events from the Middle Ages.

- the Muslim invasion
- the Reconquista

Event map

- What happened?
- When did it happen?
- How did it happen?
- Why did it happen?
- Who was involved in the event?
- Where did it happen?

2. Read the text below (A). Then read the text about the Hajj (B) on page 154. Decide if the sentences below refer to text A, B or both.

The Way of St. James (*Camino de Santiago*) was one of the most important Christian pilgrimages in the Middle Ages. In the 9th century, the remains of St. James the Apostle were discovered in northwest Spain. The legend says that after his death in Jerusalem, his remains were carried by boat to Spain and buried. After the discovery of the relics, a church was built over the tomb. The news spread quickly and Christians from all over Europe started making pilgrimages to the tomb of St. James.

a. This is a pilgrimage to a place in Saudi Arabia.

b. This pilgrimage is associated with one of the Apostles.

c. This pilgrimage has a very long history.

d. This is an important event for religious people.

e. More than 1 billion people make this pilgrimage every year.

3. Find out more about the Way of St. James. Why was it important during the Reconquista?

Review

1 In your notebook, complete the sentences by choosing the correct words.

a. *Muslim/Visigoth* society consisted of a king, nobles and peasants.
b. The name for the social organisation during the Middle Ages was *feudalism/taifas.*
c. The Kingdom of Granada was the last territory under *Muslim/Visigoth* rule.
d. The main artistic styles in medieval Spain were Islamic, *Roman/Romanesque*, Gothic and Mudéjar styles.

2 Put the events in chronological order.

a. The Reconquista finished.
b. Muslims from North Africa invaded Spain.
c. The Caliphate of Córdoba divided into taifas.
d. The Reconquista started.
e. The Visigoths settled in Hispania.
f. King Fernando II of Aragón and Queen Isabel I of Castilla married.

3 Who do the sentences below refer to?

a. They lived in castles.
b. They fought in the nobles' armies.
c. He ruled the country.
d. They worked on land belonging to the nobles.
e. They lived either in convents or monasteries.

4 Classify the characteristics listed below according to the style.

- horseshoe arches
- pointed arches
- thick walls
- stained-glass windows
- small windows
- mosaics

5 In your notebook, decide whether the following places belong to a Muslim city (**M**), a medieval Christian city (**C**) or both (**B**).

- medina
- mezquita
- alcazaba
- town hall
- protective walls
- market place
- alcázar
- cathedral

6 Talk about the Middle Ages in Spain. Use the table to help you.

- Middle Ages in Spain
  - Visigothic Spain
  - Al-Andalus
    - parts of city
    - advances/ inventions
  - Christian Kingdoms
    - parts of city
    - social organisation
    - Reconquista

7 Complete the summary on page 155.

Checklist

- I can identify the main periods of the Middle Ages.
- I can give some examples of Muslim and Christian monuments in Spain.
- I can explain the stages of the Reconquista.
- I can describe Muslim and medieval cities.
- I can explain how medieval society was organised.

8 Spain in the 15th and 16th centuries

① Read and discover.

In 1492, Christopher Columbus discovered America. This year is considered to be the beginning of the Modern Age. It was a time of discovery when people's ideas about the world changed. Explorers discovered new lands and routes around the world and brought back products that had not been seen in Europe before. As a result, sea trade flourished and Spain became a rich and important power.
What were the names of Columbus' ships?

2. Look at the smallest image. What products did explorers bring to Europe?
3. Why is the year 1492 considered the beginning of the Modern Age?
4. What was the period before the Modern Age called?
5. What problems and dangers did the explorers face during their voyages?
6. Who lived in America before the Europeans discovered them?
7. What were the consequences of the discovery of America? Think of the positive and negative consequences.
8. What do you think maps looked like before the discovery of America?

Analyse and organise

1 The discovery of America initiated the exchange of plants and animals between the continents. Copy the chart into your notebook and write **A** for America or **E** for Europe.

	origin		origin
pumpkin	.....	pineapple	.....
vanilla	.....	onion	.....
honeybee	.....	potato	.....
grape	.....	tomato	.....
turkey	.....	banana	.....
tobacco	.....	horse	.....

2 Look at the map and identify the plants and animals from Activity 1. Then name the other items. Think of other things that were exchanged between the continents.

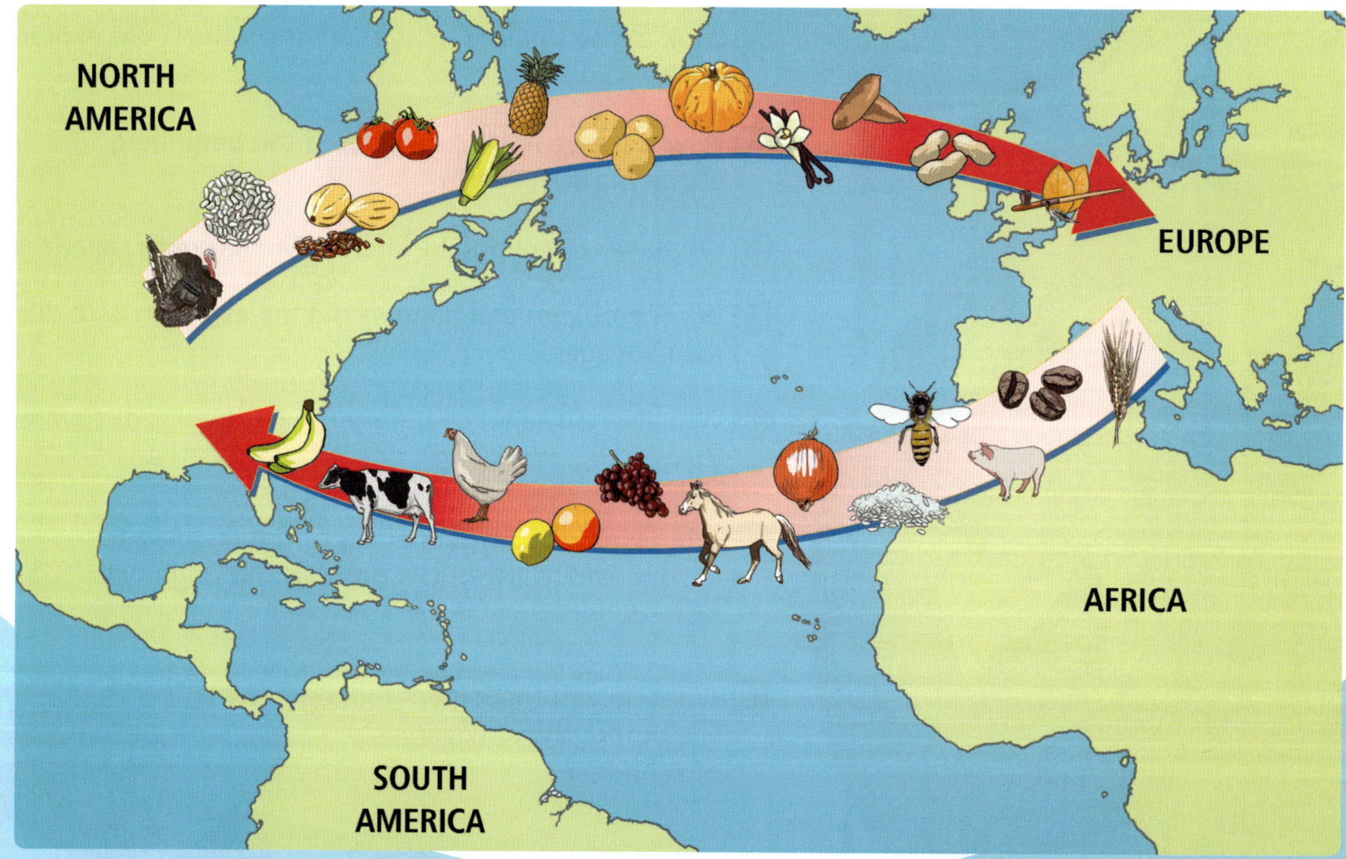

3 Read the text and decide if the sentences below are true or false.

When the Spanish arrived in America, they found a great variety of people. These were usually small tribes, but some groups had created big empires. The Spanish expeditions invaded their territories, imposing their language, culture, religion and customs.

The **Mayas** were organised as powerful city-states. They lived in Central America, in a region that is today Mexico, Belize, Guatemala and Honduras. They were the only American civilisation that developed an advanced writing system. They were also very advanced in Sciences such as astronomy, medicine and mathematics.

A Mayan temple

The **Aztecs** were governed by an emperor. They lived in the region that is today known as central Mexico. Their life was centred around religion. To honour their gods, they built temples in the shape of a pyramid. Most Aztecs were farmers. They cultivated corn, vanilla and tomatoes.

The **Incas** lived in South America, in the region that is now called Peru. Their capital city was Cuzco and their language Quechua. The Incas built a system of roads and used llamas to transport goods.

An Aztec temple

a. The Spanish conquerors found native people in the new territories.

b. It was a gradual and peaceful invasion.

c. The Incas were good astronomers.

d. Religion was very important for the Aztecs.

e. The Mayas used animals to transport food.

Llamas

4 Listen to the recording and complete the table in your notebook.

name	......
location	......
height above sea level	......
built	......
abandoned	......
rediscovered	......

The Catholic Monarchs

How was the Iberian Peninsula divided in the Middle Ages?

Isabel I of Castilla and **Fernando II of Aragón** received the title of **Catholic Monarchs** from the Pope after conquering the Kingdom of Granada. During their reign they unified the Iberian Peninsula, reinforced royal authority and imposed the Catholic religion.

The unification of Spain

The Early Modern Age in Spain began with the marriage of **Isabel I** and **Fernando II**. In 1479, they united the Kingdom of Castilla and of Aragón and created one large, powerful Christian kingdom. Then, in **1492**, they conquered the **Kingdom of Granada**. This was the end of the Reconquista. Later on they expanded their territories conquering the Kingdom of Navarra and the Canary Islands.

The unification of Spain

Link it up

What civilisations lived on the Iberian Peninsula in the Middle Ages?

Look at Unit 7.

Reforms

- The monarchy took control of the army, economy and government.
- Power was centralised. The monarchs took privileges away from the nobility and the Church.
- A strong, modern army was built to fight for the country and control its economy.
- There was an increasing interest in territorial **expansion** and **exploration**.
- Strong alliances with other European countries were established.
- The **Spanish Inquisition** was established. Its aim was to punish people who didn't follow the rules established by the Catholic Church.

The expulsion of the Jews

The year 1492

Conquest of the Kingdom of Granada

- The Kingdom of Granada was the last Muslim kingdom in Spain. It included Granada, Málaga and Almería.
- It was weakened by internal disputes, and was finally conquered by the Catholic Monarchs in 1492.

Discovery of America

- The conquest of Granada allowed the Catholic Monarchs to focus on exploration.
- Isabel and Fernando met Christopher Columbus and finally accepted his proposal asking them to sponsor his trip to find a new route to India and China.

Did you know?

The first Spanish grammar book was published in 1492 by Antonio de Nebrija.

Why was this book important?

Intolerance

- Jews and Muslims lived with Christians making important contributions to Science, music and literature.
- The Catholic Monarchs ordered Jews and Muslims to convert to the Catholic religion. The Muslims who did so were called **Moriscos**. Then the Catholic Monarchs ordered the expulsion of the Jews from Spain in 1492.

1. Decide if the following sentences refer to the Middle Ages or the Catholic Monarchs.
   a. The army was controlled by the monarchs.
   b. The nobility had a lot of power.
   c. The country didn't have a strong army.
   d. Territorial expansion was an important part of Spain's politics.
2. Why is the year 1492 so important in Spain's history? Were all the events that happened in 1492 positive?
3. Find out more about the Spanish Inquisition. How did it promote intolerance? What consequences did it have?

The discovery of America

Did Columbus ever realise he had discovered a new continent?

European countries wanted new **trade routes** to reach Asia and its silk, precious stones and spices, such as pepper and nutmeg. They wanted to find trade routes by sea instead of by land, as this was a much faster way to travel.

Christopher Columbus

Christopher Columbus was an Italian navigator and explorer. He wanted to find a new sea route to Asia. Other navigators sailed around the coast of Africa but Columbus decided to sail **west** across the Atlantic Ocean because he was convinced this was a shorter route.

The **Catholic Monarchs** financed his expedition, which led to the discovery of a new continent from a European point of view. Columbus promised to bring back gold, spices, and silks from the Far East, to spread Christianity, and later on to lead an expedition to China.

On **3 August 1492** the three **caravels** (the Santa María, the Pinta and the Niña) left Palos de la Frontera, Huelva, and on **12 October 1492** arrived in San Salvador, an island in the Bahamas.

On his **first voyage**, Columbus thought he had reached India and for this reason he called the inhabitants **Indians**. Although he made three more voyages, he died not knowing that the continent was not Asia but America.

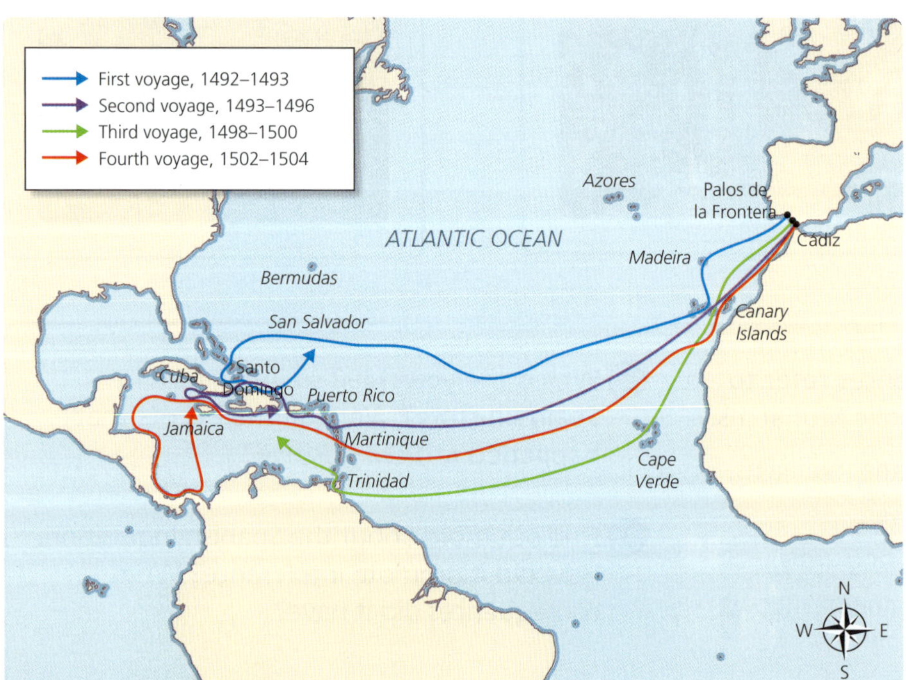

Did you know?

Caravels were faster than other ships because they were smaller and lighter. They also had square sails which could catch more wind.

What inventions helped sailors explore oceans without getting lost? Who invented them?

Spain after colonising America

- Spanish ports, such as Sevilla, grew in importance and the ship-building industry developed as a result of a greater demand for ships.
- Spain **exported goods** such as cloth, wool and leather, which meant that craftspeople also became richer. Spain also exported goods such as flour, cereals, oil and wine that could travel the long distance to America. Many farmers changed the way they farmed their land in order to produce these goods for export.
- Spain **imported** many products from America, such as new fruit and vegetables, but two of the most important raw materials from America were **gold** and **silver**. This made Spain the most powerful country in Europe.

Did you know?

In 1519, Ferdinand Magellan undertook an expedition that lasted for three years. This was the first expedition to sail around the world. He sailed across the Atlantic Ocean until he found a passage to the Pacific Ocean. It is now called the Strait of Magellan.

What was the name of a well-known Spaniard who sailed with Magellan?

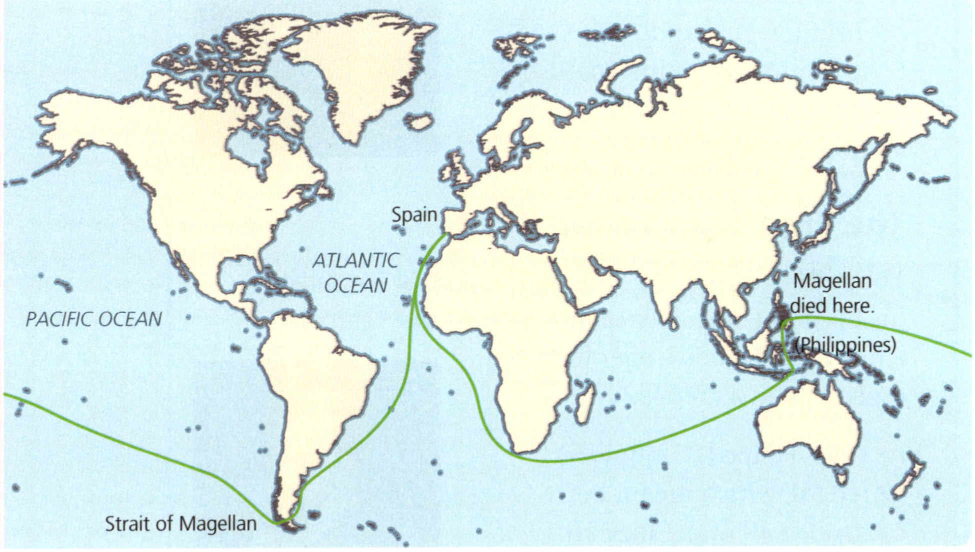

1. Explain why Columbus wanted to find a new sea route to Asia.
2. Why did Isabel and Fernando pay for Columbus' voyage?
3. What would have happened if another European country had paid for Columbus' expedition?
4. How did the discovery of America affect craftspeople and farmers in Spain?
5. Did the colonisation of America mean that Spain became richer? Why?
6. Find out where the name *America* came from.

The Spanish Empire

Throughout the 16th century, **Carlos I** and **Felipe I**, descendants of the Catholic Monarchs, ruled the most powerful empire in the world, with territories in Africa, America, Asia and Europe.

The Empire of Carlos I

Carlos I became king in 1516. He was the first Spanish king of the **Habsburg dynasty**. He ruled over a great empire, which included Spain and its territories in America. He also inherited the German Empire from his father's family. For this reason, he was also called Carlos V of Germany. His personal and national motto was *Plus Ultra* which means 'Further beyond'.

Before Carlos I died, he divided his empire into two kingdoms. He gave his German Empire to his brother, Fernando. His son, Felipe II, inherited his Spanish Empire, which included Spain and the Netherlands.

The Empire of Felipe II

Felipe II became king in 1556. In 1561, he established his permanent residence in **Madrid**. The Spanish empire **expanded** under his reign, especially in America.

In **1580**, Felipe II conquered **Portugal**, which meant he controlled all of the Iberian Peninsula and also ruled over the Portuguese territories in America, Africa and Asia.

The reign of Felipe II was also a period of wars and conflicts. Felipe II's armies won many important battles on land and at sea. In **1571**, in the **Battle of Lepanto**, the Spanish fleet stopped the Turkish Empire from taking control of the Mediterranean Sea. However, these wars were very expensive, so the king had to use gold and silver brought from America to pay for them. The price of some products increased and the Spanish population became poorer.

What is the national motto of the Kingdom of Spain?

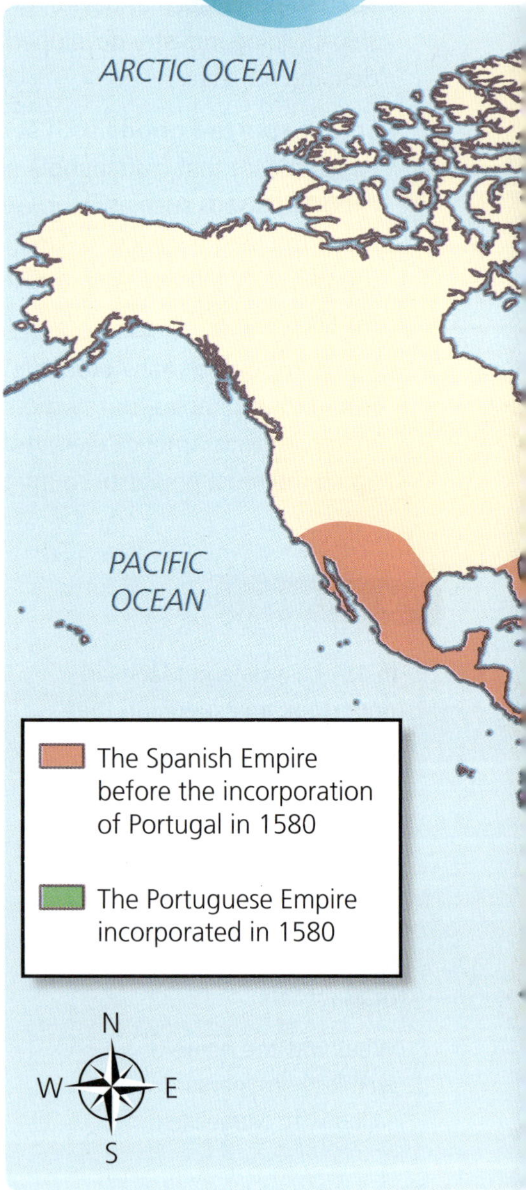

Problems in the 16th century

- controlling the new territories in America
- internal revolts in Spain
- wars in Europe
- war against the Turks

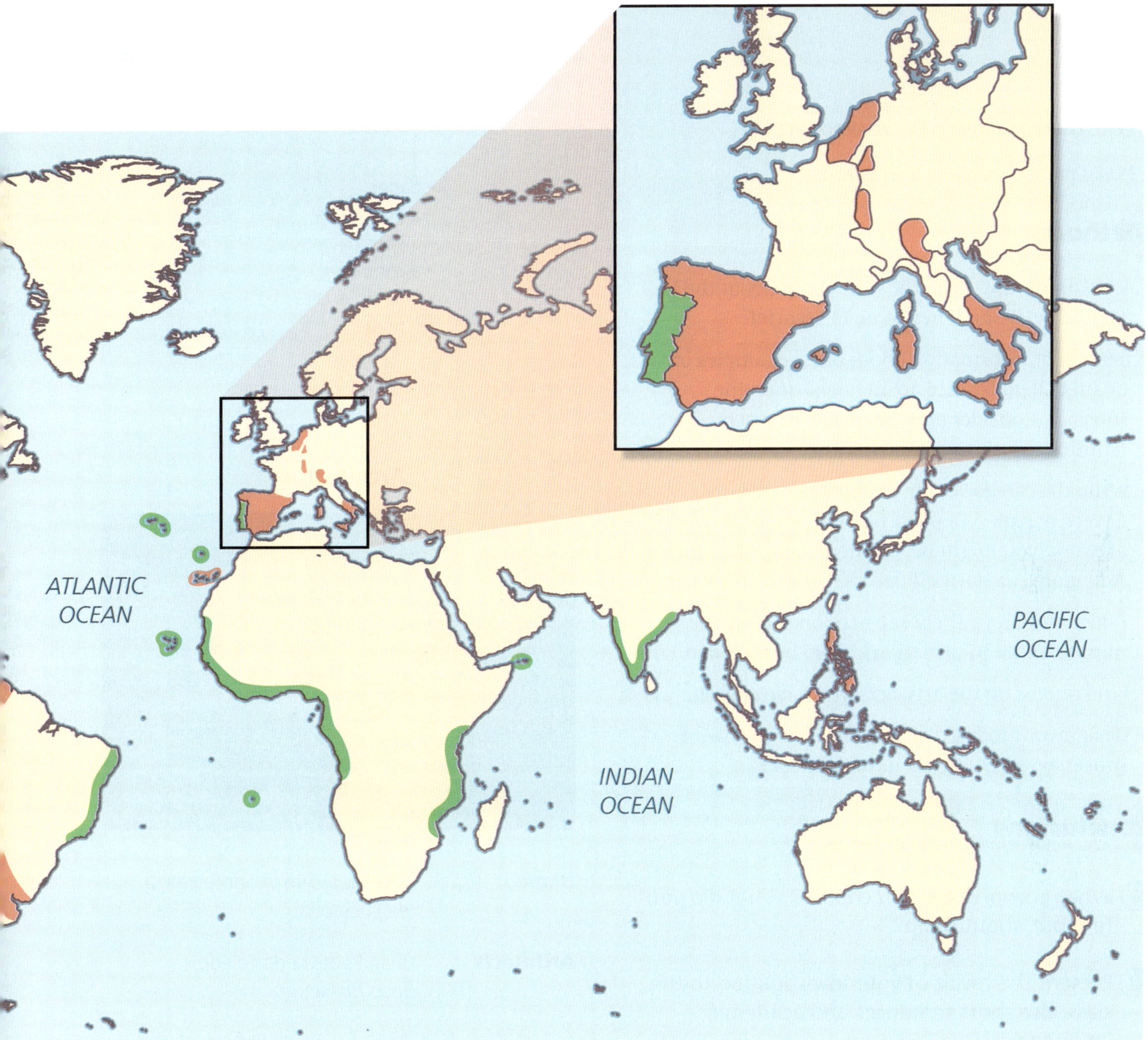

1. Why was Carlos I of Spain also called Carlos V of Germany?

2. What events happened during their reign? In your notebook, write **C** for Carlos I or **F** for Felipe II.

a. the king of Portugal
b. the court in Madrid
c. the king of Germany
d. the Battle of Lepanto
e. the invincible army
f. *Plus Ultra*

Did you know?

In 1588, Felipe II tried to invade Britain, but lost his invincible navy instead.

What was the Spanish navy called?

SCIENCE PROJECT: Spanish Renaissance

Aims

- Learn about Spanish Renaissance art.
- Make paper or digital index cards.

Method

1. Work in groups. Read the index card about the Royal Site of San Lorenzo de El Escorial.
2. Search for information about other examples of Spanish Renaissance art in books or on the Internet. Consider other forms of art, such as painting, music or sculpture.
3. Write the categories for your index cards on a piece of paper. Depending on the type of artwork, you might need different categories. Add more categories if necessary.
4. Take notes on your chosen artworks. Only the most relevant information should be recorded.
5. Find photos on the artworks you have chosen.
6. Design your index cards on paper or on a word processor. Illustrate them with images.

- paper
- a pen
- a pencil
- a computer
- Internet access
- a printer

Conclusions

1. What artworks did you choose? What did you find out about them?
2. Present the result of your investigation to the class. Use short sentences and academic language.
3. Give ideas on how to conserve and protect different forms of art.
4. Explain why your chosen artworks are important. Consider the following questions:
   a. What does the artwork tell us about the artistic style of the period?
   b. What can we learn about the personality or beliefs of the artist through this artwork?
   c. What historical information does the artwork contain?

Architecture

Name	The Royal Site of San Lorenzo de El Escorial
Architects	Juan Bautista de Toledo, Juan de Herrera
Location	San Lorenzo de El Escorial, Madrid
Commissioned by	Felipe II
Date of construction	1563–1584
Sections	The Basilica, the Royal Crypt, the Library, the Monastery
Function	Royal residence, monastery, burial crypt

Renaissance in Europe

The **Renaissance** was a cultural movement that developed in Italy before spreading throughout Europe. During the Renaissance, there was an explosion of new ideas in education and art. The artists, writers and scholars of the Renaissance looked for inspiration in Ancient Greece and Rome. Leonardo da Vinci, Michelangelo, Raphael, Jan van Eyck and Albrecht Dürer created some of the greatest artworks of the period.

The School of Athens, Raphael

Pietà, Michelangelo

Spanish Renaissance

The Renaissance spread to Spain in the 15th and 16th centuries. The beginning of the Spanish Renaissance coincided with the discovery of America, the unification of the Christian Kingdoms and the publication of the first grammar book of the Spanish language by Antonio de Nebrija. Some of the greatest artists of the Spanish Renaissance are:

- El Greco (painter);
- Juan Bautista de Toledo (architect);
- Garcilaso de la Vega, Fray Luis de León (poets);
- Teresa de Ávila, San Juan de la Cruz (mystic poets).

El entierro del señor de Orgaz (The burial of the Count of Orgaz), El Greco

1. In 1450, Johannes Gutenberg invented the printing press. How do you think it influenced the way the ideas from the Renaissance spread around Europe?
2. Find out more about Leonardo da Vinci. What else did he do besides painting?
3. Choose two Renaissance painters and search for examples of their work. What did they paint?
4. Name the three events that marked the beginning of the Spanish Renaissance. Explain why they were important.
5. Find out more about Spanish Renaissance poets mentioned in the text. What did they write about? What was mystic poetry?
6. What do we call places where paintings and sculptures are conserved and displayed? Explain why such places are important.

Revise

Study skills

1 In your notebook, order the events and write the dates. Then, make a timeline about the Spanish Empire in the 15th and 16th centuries.

- the Battle of Lepanto
- the discovery of America
- the capital city in Madrid
- the conquest of Portugal
- the conquest of Granada
- the beginning of Carlos I's reign
- the expulsion of the Jews
- the beginning of Felipe II's reign

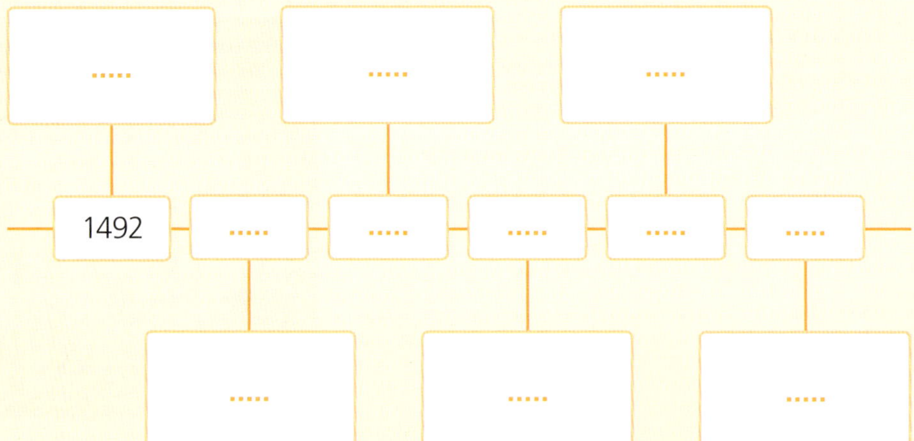

2 **Read the text below. In your notebook, complete column A with the information about Hernán Cortés. Then read the text about Francisco Pizarro (B) on page 154 and complete column B.**

Hernán Cortés was a Spanish conqueror from Medellín, Extremadura. He was born in 1485 and grew up in a good family. In 1504, he left for the New World. He spent some years in Hispaniola and Cuba. Then, in 1518, he took part in an expedition to the mainland of Mexico.

When Cortés arrived at the Yucatan Peninsula, he made friends with some native people, including the Indian princess doña Marina. They helped him with the conquest of the Aztec Empire.

In 1521, Cortés and his men destroyed Tenochtitlan, the sacred capital of the Aztecs, and killed Montezuma, their emperor. He rebuilt Tenochtitlan as the Spanish city of Mexico. After the conquest of Mexico was completed, he became the governor of these new territories.

	A	B
name	.....	.....
place of birth	.....	.....
date of birth	.....	.....
conquered	.....	.....
destroyed	.....	.....
founded	.....	.....

Review

1 Read the sentences. Which monarch's reign do they refer to?

a. The Jews were expelled from Spain.
b. Christopher Columbus discovered America.
c. Portugal was conquered.
d. Wars with the Turks took place.
e. The Spanish fleet won at the Battle of Lepanto.
f. The Spanish population became poorer because of the high costs of wars.

2 Look at the map. What event does it illustrate? Complete the table in your notebook.

When did it begin?	.....
Where did it begin?	.....
Where did it end?	.....
How long did it last?	.....
Who paid for it?	.....
Who organised it?	.....
What means of transport was involved?	.....
What were the consequences?	.....

3 Classify the words in the box. Add two words to each group.

cocoa bean cow banana tobacco
honeybee cereals corn grape
vanilla rice horse pumpkin

- Spanish Empire
  - export
    - .....
  - import
    - .....

4 Talk about the discovery of America. Use the sentences to help you.

- European countries wanted to find new sea trade routes to .....
- Spain became richer due to .....
- Spanish ports .....
- Spain ..... products, such as bananas, ...
- It also ..... products, such as gold, ...

5 Complete the summary on page 155.

Checklist

- I can list the most important events that occurred in the Spanish Empire in the 15th and 16th centuries.
- I can explain the importance of the discovery of America.
- I can enumerate territories that belonged to the Spanish Empire in the 16th century.

9 Spain in the 17th and 18th centuries

① Read and discover.

In the 17th century, the Spanish Empire entered a gradual economic decline. The numerous causes of this crisis included expensive wars, plagues and dependence on gold and silver imported from America. The 18th century began with the War of Succession. As a result, Spain lost part of its territories in Europe. The Habsburg dynasty was replaced by the Bourbon dynasty. Who was the first king of the Bourbon dynasty?

2. What event ended the reign of the Habsburg dynasty in Spain?

3. Look at the largest image and answer the questions.
   - Do you think all these people belong to the same social class? Why?
   - Do you think life was easy in the 17th and 18th centuries? Why?

4. What do the two smaller images show? What social class do you associate them with? Why?

5. What differences can you see between the society shown in the largest image and the contemporary society? Consider the following:
   - clothes
   - transport
   - free time
   - work

Analyse and organise

1. The main artistic styles of the Early Modern Age in Spain were the Renaissance and Baroque. Find out more and, in your notebook, complete the table.

• Toledo • movement • Velázquez • contrast • symmetry • Greco

	Spanish Renaissance	Spanish Baroque
time	• 15th and 16th centuries	• 17th and 18th centuries
characteristics	• harmony • frozen moment, rest • natural and balanced colours • ....., balance, proportions	• dramatic and emotional • action and ..... • ..... between light and dark colours • elaborate ornamentation
artists	• El ..... • Luis de Morales • Juan Bautista de	• Diego ..... • Francisco de Zurbarán • Bartolomé Esteban Murillo

2. Look at the photos. Use the characteristics from Activity 1 to classify the works of art in the photos. Find out more and name the paintings and the monuments.

a

b

c

d

e

f

3 Read the text. Choose the best word for each space.

The Early Modern Age started in Spain with the discovery of America and finished in the late 18th century. During this time, social structure was hierarchical and very (1) ..... Social classes were based on status and wealth. It was very difficult to move up from one class to another. Society was divided between the privileged class and the unprivileged class.

Privileged class

- All power was held by the **monarch**.
- **Nobles** and **clergy** were very (2) ..... and rich. They didn't have to pay taxes and owned most of the land. Nobles and bishops lived in (3) ....., in mansions or at the court. Monks and priests led simpler lives.

Unprivileged class

Most people belonged to the unprivileged class.

- The **middle class** included bankers, merchants, craftspeople, lawyers and (4) .....
- The **lower class** was made up of poor people who worked all day for a very low salary.

1 a. unfair b. good c. fair
2 a. poor b. influential c. expensive
3 a. castles b. monasteries c. houses
4 a. kings b. doctors c. slaves

4 Listen to the recording about society in the Early Modern Age. In your notebook, complete the missing information.

- The population of the Early Modern Age was mostly .....
- Living conditions in villages were very .....
- Peasants lived in small houses with no .....
- In towns and cities, rich people lived in comfortable .....
- The streets in cities were usually ....., because there were no sewage systems.

Spain in the 17th century

Why did pirates attack Spanish ships?

Constant wars in the previous century and the cost of maintaining a large empire had many consequences for Spain in the 17th century. A great economic crisis began and Spain entered a difficult period of financial and political troubles.

The economic crisis

During the 17th century, Spain was involved in many wars over territory and religion, such as the **Thirty Years' War** from 1618 to 1648. By the end of the 17th century, Spain had lost some of its territories in Europe, including **Portugal**. The kings spent large amounts of money paying their soldiers and the officials involved in the administration of the Spanish Empire. This left less gold and silver for other purposes. In addition, pirates, often supported by France or England, attacked Spanish ships on their way back to Spain from America.

Three **Habsburg** kings ruled during the 17th century. They were: **Felipe III**, **Felipe IV** and **Carlos II**. These kings allowed ministers to represent them and to control government administration. These ministers, called *validos*, became very powerful.

The Thirty Years' War

Felipe III

Felipe III was king between 1598 and 1621. Under his rule, Spain started to lose power and influence in Europe.

Felipe started to leave his power in the hands of *validos*, who became the real rulers of the country. The Duque de Lerma, had a lot of power during Felipe III's reign.

Economic problems soon started to build up. Gold and silver were not arriving in such large quantities from America, the country was not in good hands and previously prosperous cities such as Segovia, Toledo and Sevilla started to undergo a slow economic decline.

Felipe IV

Felipe IV was king between 1621 and 1665, but in reality his *valido,* the Conde-Duque de Olivares ruled the country for him. In 1640, Portugal revolted, which led to **Portugal's independence** from the Spanish Empire in **1668**.

Carlos II

Carlos II ruled between 1665 and 1700. He couldn't have any children. The Habsburg dynasty in Spain ended in **1700** when Carlos II died without an heir.

Social problems

The population of Spain decreased during the 17th century. Many people died in wars. Famine, caused by poor harvests and plagues, also reduced the population.

Many people emigrated to America to find a better life. In the meantime, the population of **Moriscos** was increasing in Spain. Some Moriscos were successful merchants and shopkeepers. Due to this increase in power, the decision was made to expel the Moriscos from Spain. Many children were separated from their families, as their parents left Spain.

The expulsion of the Moriscos

1. How was 17th-century Spain different from 16th-century Spain?
2. Explain the main causes of the economic crisis in 17th-century Spain.
3. Explain why the 17th century was a time of decline for Spain.
4. Explain the changes that occurred in the Spanish population in the 17th century.
5. What happens if a king dies without an heir?

Link it up

Who was expelled from Spain in the 16th century?

Look at Unit 8.

The Golden Age

Think of some examples of Spanish art from the Renaissance.

The **Golden Age** was a period of great achievement in Spanish art. It was a time when many great works of art and literature were created. It coincided with the voyages of Columbus and the rise and decline of the Spanish Habsburg dynasty. The main styles of the Golden Age were the **Renaissance** and the **Baroque**.

Baroque painting

The famous Baroque painters of the Golden Age were **Velázquez**, **Ribera**, **Zurbarán** and **Murillo**. The main features of their style were realism and the way in which they transmitted emotion.

Diego Rodríguez de Silva y Velázquez

Velázquez painted portraits of Felipe IV and the royal family, and historical scenes. Some of his best paintings are portraits of the royal children.

La rendición de Breda (The Surrender of Breda). 1635

José de Ribera

Ribera's painting style was called **tenebrism** because his paintings show a strong contrast of dark and light.

San Jerónimo (Saint Jerome). 17th century

Francisco de Zurbarán

Zurbarán specialised in still lifes and religious paintings of monks, nuns and martyrs.

Bodegón (Still Life). 1650

Bartolomé Esteban Murillo

Murillo is best known for portraits of women and children, as well as religious scenes.

Mujeres en la ventana (A Girl and her Duenna). 1675

Baroque architecture

During the Golden Age, many beautiful churches and squares were built.

La Clerecía, Salamanca

The Cathedral of Murcia

The Plaza Mayor in Salamanca

The Plaza Mayor in Madrid

Baroque literature

During the Golden Age, brilliant writers created great literary works. The printing press, invented in 1450, helped to distribute their works.

- **theatre**: Félix Lope de Vega, Tirso de Molina, Pedro Calderón de la Barca
- **poetry**: Francisco de Quevedo, Luis de Góngora
- **novels**: Miguel de Cervantes, Baltasar Gracián

Félix Lope de Vega

1. Find out more about the painters. In your notebook, complete the table.

	Murillo	Zurbarán	Ribera
place of birth	......	......	......
main themes	......	......	......
three examples	......	......	......

2. Choose two writers from the Golden Age and find out more about them. What are some examples of their works? What were their main themes?

Spain in the 18th century

Why was there a war of succession in Spain?

The 18th century was a time of many changes in the political and social structure of Spain. The Spanish economy improved and the population increased, with many people moving to towns and cities.

The Spanish War of Succession

Carlos II died in 1700 leaving no heir to the throne. Two royal families claimed the Spanish throne: the French **Bourbons** and the Austrian **Habsburgs**. This dispute developed into the **Spanish War of Succession**, which lasted from 1701 until 1714. This war started as a civil war and then expanded into an international war.

The war ended with the signing of the **Treaty of Utrecht**, and the Bourbon dynasty replaced the Habsburgs. **Felipe V** became the king of Spain, but in exchange, Spain lost some of its territories in Europe. The Spanish territories in the Netherlands and Italy were given to Austria, and Gibraltar and Menorca were given to the British.

The Battle of Almansa, 1707

Europe after the Treaty of Utrecht

Felipe V

Felipe V established a new form of government called an **absolute monarchy**. This means that the monarch has unlimited power. Felipe V also centralised the government and created new laws for the whole Empire.

Did you know?

Jorge Juan y Santacilia was a Spanish mathematician and scientist. He discovered the fact that the Earth is not perfectly spherical, but flattened at the poles.

Find out more about the expeditions that helped Jorge Juan come to such conclusions.

The Enlightenment

A period known as the **Enlightenment** brought significant cultural changes to some countries in Europe during the 18th century. At the centre of the Enlightenment was a belief in human reason over religion or authority. People began to believe that they could improve their lives through education or involvement in politics. In Spain, the Enlightenment coincided with the reign of Felipe V and his successors: Fernando VI, Carlos III and Carlos IV. The Royal Botanical Garden of Madrid was founded during the Enlightenment.

Carlos III

Carlos III did a lot to modernise Spain. Cities became more hygienic and safer thanks to new sewage systems, water systems, street lighting and pavements. Carlos III created hospitals, museums and botanical gardens. Streets became wider and fountains and monuments were built. Carlos III also supported the development of industry, agriculture and trade.

The court of Carlos IV

The court painter **Francisco de Goya** recorded the events of the end of the 18th century in Spain. He started painting the royal family of Carlos III in 1785 and continued to paint during Carlos IV's reign. With an explosion of light and colour, Goya's portraits show the splendour and wealth of the royal family. However, in the next century, Goya's style would change.

La familia de Carlos IV
(Charles IV of Spain and His Family). 1800

1. What caused the Spanish War of Succession?
2. How did Spanish cities change in the 18th century in comparison with the previous centuries?
3. Why did the Spanish population increase during the 18th century?
4. Are there any 18th-century buildings near where you live?
5. Find out more about Francisco de Goya. What type of paintings did he create?
6. The Prado Museum was built during the reign of Carlos III. What other monuments in Madrid were created during his reign?

SCIENCE PROJECT: Analysing a painting

Aims

- Analyse a painting by Goya.
- Study the historical time period through the painting.
- Make paper or digital index cards.

- a printer
- paper
- a pen
- a computer
- Internet access

Hypothesis

I think that Goya's paintings ...

- have a social or political message, or
- don't have a social or political message.

Method

1. Work in groups. Read the index card about the painting *La vendimia* by Goya.
2. Find two other paintings by Goya and search for information about them.
3. On a piece of paper write the categories for your index cards.
4. Take notes on your chosen paintings. Only the most relevant information should be recorded. Pay special attention to:
   - people's clothes and physical appearance;
   - what they are doing;
   - the objects they are holding.
5. Design your index cards on paper or on a word processor. Illustrate them with images.
6. Choose one of the paintings. Write a short text about the scene represented and its main theme.
7. Present the text to the class.

Painter	Francisco de Goya y Lucientes
Title	*La vendimia (The Grape Harvest)*
Year	1786
Scene	Aristocrats enjoying themselves and farmers working
Theme	Allegory of autumn; social message
Features	Layered composition with different scenes in the background and foreground

Conclusions

1. What painting did you choose? What did you find out about it?
2. Present the results of your investigation to the class. Use short sentences and academic language.
3. What social group do the people depicted in the paintings belong to? How do you know?
4. What else can you learn about life in the Early Modern Age by looking at the paintings?

FRAGILE WORLD: The poor and the rich

In the Early Modern Age, the world was divided into two unequal parts: the privileged and the unprivileged. The great artists of this time portrayed these two different worlds.

The poor

Although **Murillo** is best known for his religious work, his paintings of street life in Sevilla give us a visual record of the everyday life of his time. Here we can see the misery of homeless children.

Niños comiendo uvas y melón (Beggar Boys Eating Grapes and Melon). 1650

Los niños jugando a los dados (Boys Playing Dice). 1675

The rich

Velázquez portrayed the members of the royal family and other wealthy people in many paintings. Their clothes and appearance contrast greatly with the poor people on the streets. Here princess Margarita and prince Baltasar pose with very luxurious clothes.

La infanta Margarita. 1654

Retrato del príncipe Baltasar Carlos. 1632

1. Look at the paintings and answer the questions.
   - **a.** Who are these children? Where are they?
   - **b.** What information can you find out about their life? Consider the following:
     - clothes
     - food
     - free time
     - education
2. Compare the paintings.
   - **a.** Are the children posing for the painter? If they are, why are they posing?
   - **b.** Does the artist paint the children in a realistic way, or does he idealise their features?
3. Are there rich and poor children in modern society? How does today compare with past centuries?

Revise

Study skills

1 In your notebook, complete the diagram. What event marked the change of the two dynasties?

- Felipe V
- cultural advance
- Golden Age
- Thirty Years' War
- *validos*
- modernisation of Spain
- Carlos II
- Carlos III
- population increase
- population decrease
- expulsion of the Moriscos
- Enlightenment

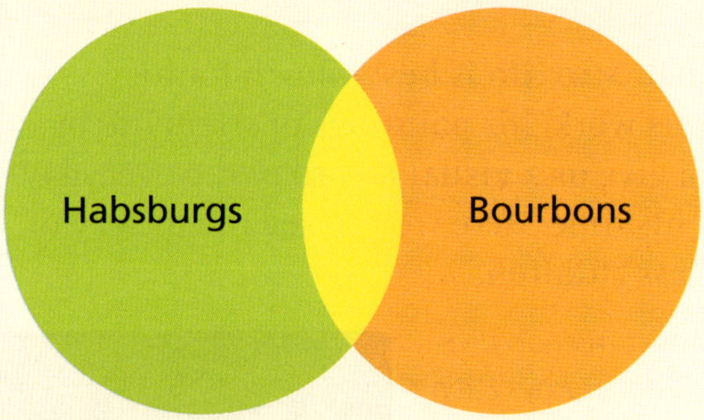

2 Read the text below. In your notebook, complete column A with the information about Velázquez. Then read the text about Cervantes (B) on page 154 and complete column B.

Diego Rodríguez de Silva y Velázquez was a very famous painter from the Spanish Golden Age. He was born in Sevilla in 1599. When he was 11, he told his parents that he wanted to be a painter. He moved to Madrid and very soon became a portrait artist in the court of king Felipe IV. He was the king's painter until he died.

His delicate painting style and the harmony of light and colours he used made him a famous painter of his time. He influenced many artists in the following centuries. One of his most famous paintings is *Las Meninas* (*The Maids of Honour*). Other painters admired his work, but some were jealous of his position. Velázquez died in Madrid in 1660, aged 61.

	A	B
profession	.....	.....
birth	.....	Alcalá de Henares, 1547
death	Madrid, 1660	.....
problems	Other painters were jealous of him.	.....
most famous piece of work	.....	.....

Review

1 Read the sentences. In your notebook, write the names of the kings they refer to. Which dynasty did each king belong to?

a. The real power belonged to the Conde-Duque de Olivares.
b. Goya painted a portrait of his family.
c. He died without an heir.
d. He introduced the absolute monarchy.
e. He introduced various improvements in Spanish cities.

2 Decide if the following events occurred in the 17th or 18th century. In your notebook, complete the table.

a. The War of Succession took place.
b. Ministers called *validos* ruled the country.
c. The Treaty of Utrecht was signed.
d. Many Spaniards emigrated to America.
e. Spain lost Gibraltar.

17th century	18th century
.....	.....

3 In your notebook, order the events from the earliest to the most recent. Write the dates.

a. The Spanish War of Succession began.
b. Felipe V became the first Bourbon king of Spain.
c. The Thirty Years' War began.
d. Carlos II died.
e. Portugal became independent.

4 How do you think these events contributed to the economic and political crisis in Spain?

a. Pirates attacked Spanish ships.
b. Spain was involved in many wars.
c. The country was ruled by *validos*.
d. The Spanish population decreased.

5 Complete the diagram in your notebook.

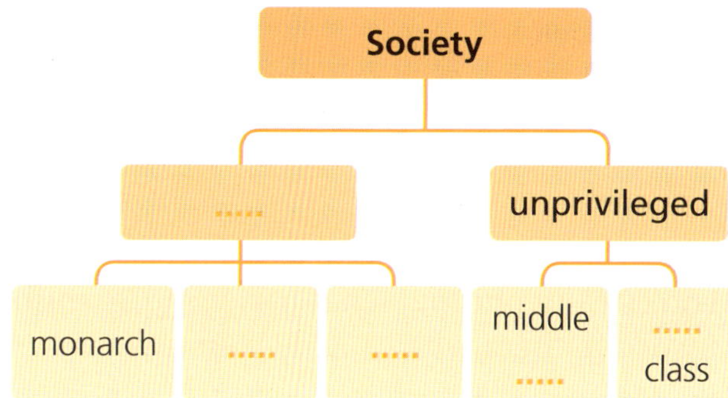

6 Read the sentences. Who do they refer to?

a. His style of painting was called tenebrism.
b. He painted the family of Felipe IV.
c. He painted the family of Carlos IV.
d. They were famous poets from the Golden Age.

7 Talk about Spain in the 17th and 18th centuries. Use the sentences to help you.

- In the 17th century, Spain was involved in .....
- It also suffered a ..... crisis, because kings' ..... had too much power.
- As a result, the Spanish population .....
- In the 18th century, the Spanish economy .....

8 Complete the summary on page 155.

Checklist

- I can list the most important events in Spain in the 17th and 18th centuries.
- I can list the main artists from the Spanish Golden Age.
- I can explain the causes of the crisis that Spain experienced in the 17th century.

TEAMWORK Spain's history

1 **Are these statements true or false? Correct the false ones in your notebook.**

a. The Middle Ages began when the Roman Empire fell in AD 496.

b. The Visigoths first arrived on the Iberian Peninsula before the Roman Empire fell.

c. The Iberian Peninsula was invaded by the Muslims.

d. The Reconquista began in the 9th century.

e. Spanish medieval art was only influenced by Christians.

2 **Look at the photos. What periods in Spanish history do you associate them with? Justify your answers.**

a

b

c

d

3 **Read and cross the odd one out. Justify your answers.**

1 Privileged groups in the Early Modern Age

a. nobles

b. lawyers

c. clergy

2 Art in the Golden Age

a. Picasso

b. Velázquez

c. Murillo

3 17th-century monarchs

a. Felipe V

b. Felipe IV

c. Carlos II

4 16th-century monarchs

a. Carlos I

b. Felipe II

c. Martin Luther

The whole is greater than the sum of its parts.

Group project

4 Look at the pictures. Order these monarchs chronologically. What important events occurred during their reigns?

a

Carlos III

b

Felipe II

c

Carlos I

d

Felipe V

5 In groups, choose one of the periods in Spain's history that you have studied. Make a poster or slide presentation. Present it to the rest of your class. Your project should include the following information:

- What is your chosen century?
- Who ruled Spain in the period you have chosen?
- What were the main events that took place in that century?
- What were the main characteristics of that century? Consider the following:
  - political stability and wars
  - economy
  - population
  - society
- Were there any battles in that century?
- What characterises the art from your chosen century?
  - architecture
  - sculpture
  - painting
  - literature

Use books or the Internet to look for pictures and extra information. Include only small amounts of information on each slide. Remember to include a reference list.

Checklist

- All group members contributed actively to the project.
- We generated ideas about how to organise the information.
- We thought of the different events that took place in our chosen century.
- We searched for new information from various sources.

Quick quiz

1. Listen to the quiz and choose the correct answer from the options.

1	a. king	b. emir	c. caliph
2	a. guilds	b. craftspeople	c. merchants
3	a. Fernando	b. Carlos I	c. Felipe II
4	a. pineapple	b. banana	c. grape
5	a. Velázquez	b. Zurbarán	c. Goya
6	a. Renaissance	b. tenebrism	c. cubism

2. Listen and check your answers.

A

B

C

D

Extended quiz

3. Read the quiz and write your ideas in your notebook.

1. When did Muslims invade the Iberian Peninsula?
2. What were the four main styles of medieval art in Spain?
3. Say which art style you can see in each of the photos A–D.
4. What did Columbus call the inhabitants of the New World?
5. When did the Spanish War of Succession end?
6. What were the two main groups in the Early Modern Age society?

4. Listen to this student's answers. Match them to questions 1 to 6 in Activity 3.

5. Now listen to the answers in order. Check your original ideas from Activity 3.

Team test!

① Get into teams. Take turns to guess the words for definitions 1–9.

Team A

1. ..... : the capital city of the Visigothic Kingdom.
2. ..... : the battle in which don Pelayo defeated the Muslims.
3. ..... : one of the styles in medieval art. The Alhambra is an example.
4. ..... : one of the Pre-Columbian civilisations. It was organised in city-states.
5. ..... : the name given to Queen Isabel and King Fernando.
6. ..... : Muslims who converted to Catholicism.
7. ..... : the last Habsburg king of Spain.
8. ..... : a period of great achievement in Spanish art and literature.
9. ..... : the king who introduced a number of improvements in Spanish cities.
10. ..... : ______________________.

Team B

1. ..... : small independent Muslim states created in the 11th century.
2. ..... : the battle in which the Visigoths were defeated. It took place in 711.
3. ..... : one of the styles in medieval art. The Cathedral of Teruel is an example.
4. ..... : one of the Pre-Columbian civilisations. Their capital city was Cuzco.
5. ..... : the last Muslim kingdom in Spain. It was conquered in 1492.
6. ..... : a small sailing ship.
7. ..... : one of the Spanish Baroque painters. He painted *Las Meninas*.
8. ..... : the king who established absolute monarchy in Spain.
9. ..... : the dynasty that replaced the Habsburgs on the throne of Spain.
10. ..... : ______________________.

② Listen and check your answers.

③ Now, in your notebook, invent a tenth definition. Ask someone from the other team to guess the words for definitions 1–10.

Study skills texts

1 The Universe

The Sun, the planets and the Moon travel along an imaginary belt called the zodiac. This belt consists of 12 constellations called zodiac constellations. These constellations appear to form different patterns in the night sky. The names of these constellations are of Greek origin. They are called Aries, Taurus, Gemini, Cancer, Leo, Virgo, Libra, Scorpio, Sagittarius, Capricorn, Aquarius and Pisces. Astrologers use these constellations as zodiacal signs. According to them, everyone has a zodiacal sign depending on the period they were born in.

2 Representing the Earth

Autonomous Community	National Park
Andalucía	Doñana National Park
	Sierra Nevada National Park
Canarias	Timanfaya National Park Teide National Park
Castilla-La Mancha	Tablas de Daimiel National Park
Asturias, Cantabria	Picos de Europa National Park
Extremadura	Monfragüe National Park

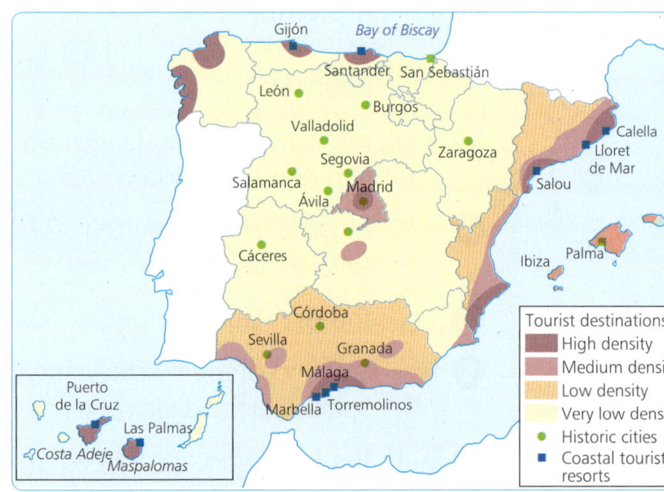

3 Climate and weather

Tornadoes usually develop from storms; they are formed when different air masses with differing temperatures meet. The colder air pushes up the warm air very quickly and forms a dark spinning column. The centre of the tornado is called a vortex. Tornadoes can travel at 500 kilometres per hour. They are so strong that they can move through an area and destroy everything in their path in minutes. They cause damage to buildings or other objects on the ground when the tip of the column reaches the ground. Tornadoes are sometimes called twisters because of the way they move.

Unit review summaries

- **Components of the Universe** (stars, planets, dwarf planets, satellites, meteoroids, meteors, meteorites, comets, asteroids)
- **The Solar System**
  - **the Sun**
  - **eight planets**: **inner** (Mercury, Venus, Earth, Mars) and **outer** (Jupiter, Saturn, Uranus, Neptune)
- **The Earth**
  - **rotation**: 24 hours (day and night)
  - **revolution**: 365 days (seasons)
- **The Moon**
  - **rotation** (28 days) and **revolution** (28 days)
  - **phases of the Moon**
  - **tides**
  - **eclipses**

- **Spheres of the Earth**
  - **atmosphere**
  - **biosphere**
  - **geosphere**: core, mantle, crust
  - **hydrosphere**
- **Geographic coordinates**
  - **parallels**: latitude (Equator)
  - **meridians**: longitude (Prime Meridian)
- **Maps**
  - **compass rose**
  - **key**
  - **scale**
- **Types of maps**
  - **political maps**
  - **physical maps**
  - **weather maps**

- **Elements of climate**
  - **temperature** (thermometer, °C or °F)
  - **humidity** (hygrometer, %)
  - **precipitation** (rain gauge, mm)
  - **wind** (anemometer, km/h)
  - **atmospheric pressure** (barometer, hPa)
- **Factors that influence climate** (latitude, landform or relief, altitude, distance from the sea)
- **Climate zones**
  - **hot**: equatorial, tropical
  - **temperate**: oceanic, continental, Mediterranean
  - **cold**: polar, alpine
  - **desert climate**
- **Climate zones in Spain** (oceanic, continental, subtropical, alpine, Mediterranean)

Study skills texts

4 Spain's politics and culture

San Isidro is one of the biggest festivals in Madrid. It is celebrated on 15 May. San Isidro is the patron saint of Madrid and also of farmers. The main celebrations are held in an open-air area called the Pradera de San Isidro where people take part in a pilgrimage to the shrine of San Isidro. People wear traditional costumes of *chulapos* and *goyescas* and celebrate by dancing the regional dance called the *chotis* and eating typical dishes like the *cocido madrileño*.

5 Spanish population

La Ribera, Ávila, looks like a ghost village today, but a long time ago, it was a vibrant village full of people and life. Up to 400 people once lived here. People in La Ribera worked on their farms and lived from agriculture and livestock. They had their festivals and celebrations and a busy social life. But from the 1960s the village started a slow but steady decline. Young people started to move to bigger towns, and most of them went to live in large urban areas, such as Madrid, where they could find good jobs and a more comfortable life. Gradually, the village lost all the young people and older people either died or left. Sadly, after a few years, La Ribera was completely abandoned.

6 Europe

Europe Day is one of the symbols of the European Union. It is celebrated on 9 May to commemorate the Schuman Declaration. The Schuman Declaration was a proposal made in 1950 to create a new type of organisation of European countries. This proposal is considered to be the beginning of the creation of the European Union. The main objective of Europe Day is to teach people about the European Union and to celebrate peace and unity in Europe. Member States celebrate Europe Day by organising different events, such as competitions, film festivals or lectures.

Unit review summaries

- **Symbols of Spain**
  - flag
  - national anthem
  - coat of arms
- **Parliamentary monarchy**
  - Felipe VI
- **Autonomous Communities** (Statute of Autonomy, institutions)
- **Spanish Constitution** (1978)
  - legislative power: Parliament (*Congreso de los Diputados, Senado*)
  - executive power: Government (*Presidente del Gobierno,* ministers)
  - judicial power: courts, tribunals
- **Rights and responsibilities of citizens**

- **Groups of population**
  - age: child, adult, elderly
  - location: urban, rural
  - economic activity: active, inactive
- **Changing population**
  - natural increase: positive, negative
  - actual increase: positive, negative
  - population density
  - causes of migratory movements
- **Spanish population**
  - inhabitants: 46 million
  - life expectancy: 81 years
  - population density: 93 inhabitants per km^2
- **Migratory movements in Spain**
  - international emigration
  - internal migration: rural exodus
  - international immigration

- **European Union**
  - members: 28 countries
  - inhabitants: over 500 million
  - population density: 117 inhabitants per km^2
  - languages: 24 official languages
- **EU history**
  - 1957: European Economic Community
  - 1993: European Union
- **EU symbols**
  - currency: euro
  - flag: 12 stars
  - anthem: *Ode to Joy*
- **EU institutions** (European Parliament, Council of the EU, European Council, European Comission, Court of Justice of the EU, European Court of Auditors)

Study skills texts

7 The Middle Ages

The Hajj is an Islamic pilgrimage to Mecca (Saudi Arabia). This is a religious duty that must be performed by every Muslim at least once in their lifetime. Every year, 1.3 billion Muslims travel to Mecca to pray and to perform some rituals. The most important of them is walking seven times around the Ka'aba, the most sacred site for Muslims.

For many centuries, tribes from all around the Arabian Peninsula travelled to Mecca, regardless of their religion. Then, in the Middle Ages, the prophet Muhammad unified the Peninsula into a single state under Islam. Since that time, the Hajj has been an Islamic pilgrimage attended only by Muslims.

8 Spain in the 15th and 16th centuries

Francisco Pizarro was the second cousin of Hernán Cortés. He was born in Trujillo, Extremadura in 1476. He sailed from Spain to America in 1502. He went on a few expeditions where he heard about the wealth of the Inca Empire. He started his conquest in 1532. The natives tried to resist his attacks, but Pizarro captured the Inca Emperor, Atahualpa. After the Incas paid the ransom, Pizarro killed the emperor and the leaders of the Inca government. As a result, the Spaniards conquered the Inca Empire. Pizarro destroyed its capital, Cuzco, and then founded the city of Lima, the capital of Peru.

9 Spain in the 17th and 18th centuries

Miguel de Cervantes Saavedra (1547–1616) was a Spanish novelist whose most important works were written in the early 17th century. He was born in Alcalá de Henares. Before beginning his career as a writer, he enrolled in the army and fought in many battles against the Turks. He participated heroically in the Battle of Lepanto where he lost his left hand. As he was sailing back to Spain, he and his brother were captured and taken prisoner by the Turks; they lived in captivity for five years. After so many adventures, he started writing novels and plays. He published his world famous *Don Quixote de la Mancha* in two parts, in 1605 and 1615. *Don Quixote* was an immediate great success and is considered the first bestselling novel in history. Cervantes died in Madrid at the age of 69.

Unit review summaries

- **Visigothic Kingdom**
  - **Visigoth society**: king, nobles, peasants
  - **culture**: examples
- **Al-Andalus**
  - **AD 711**: Muslim invasion
  - **Al-Andalus city**: medina, zoco, mezquita, alcázar, alcazaba
  - **legacy**: examples
- **Reconquista**
  - **1492**: conquest of the Kingdom of Granada
  - **medieval society**: king, nobles, knights, clergy, peasants
  - **medieval city**: walls, gateways, narrow streets, main square
- **Styles in medieval art** (Islamic, Romanesque, Gothic, Mudéjar)

- **Pre-Columbian civilisations** (Mayas, Aztecs, Incas)
- **Catholic Monarchs** (Isabel and Fernando)
  - **conquest of the Kingdom of Granada**
  - **discovery of America**
  - **expulsion of the Jews**
- **Age of discovery** (Christopher Columbus, Ferdinand Magellan, Hernán Cortés, Francisco Pizarro)
- **Spanish Empire** (Carlos I, Felipe II)
- **Golden Age** (Renaissance)
  - **in Europe**: Leonardo da Vinci, Raphael, Jan vanEyck, Albrecht Dürer
  - **in Spain**: El Greco, Juan Bautista de Toledo, Garcilaso de la Vega, Fray Luis de León, Teresa de Ávila, Juan de la Cruz

- **Early Modern society**
  - **privileged class**: king, nobles, clergy
  - **unprivileged class**: middle class (bankers, merchants, craftspeople, lawyers, doctors), lower class
- **Spain in the 17th century**
  - **economic crisis**
  - **wars**
  - **Habsburgs**: Felipe III, Felipe IV, Carlos II
- **Golden Age** (Baroque)
  - **painting**: Velázquez, Ribera, Zurbarán, Murillo
  - **architecture**
  - **literature**: theatre, poetry, novels
- **Spain in the 18th century**
  - **Spanish War of Succession**: Treaty of Utrecht
  - **Bourbons**: Felipe V, Fernando VI, Charlos III, Carlos IV